W9-BUJ-745

Differentiated Early Literacy for English Language Learners

Practical Strategies

Paul Boyd-Batstone

California State University - Long Beach

PEARSON

A and B

Boston • New York • San Francisco
Mexico City • Montreal • Toronto • London • Madrid • Munich • Paris
Hong Kong • Singapore • Tokyo • Cape Town • Sydney

To Mory Ouk,
a survivor of the Cambodian holocaust,
my student and my teacher.

Senior Series Editor: *Aurora Martínez Ramos*
Series Editorial Assistant: *Kevin Shannon and Mekea Harvey*
Executive Marketing Manager: *Krista Clark*
Production Editor: *Janet Domingo*
Editorial Production Service: *Stratford Publishing Services, Inc.*
Composition Buyer: *Linda Cox*
Manufacturing Buyer: *Andrew Turso*
Electronic Composition: *Stratford Publishing Services, Inc.*
Cover Administrator: *Joel Gendron*

For related titles and support materials, visit our online catalog at www.ablongman.com.

Copyright © 2006 Pearson Education, Inc.

All rights reserved. No part of the material protected by this copyright notice may be reproduced or utilized in any form or by any means, electronic or mechanical, including photocopying, recording, or by any information storage and retrieval system, without written permission from the copyright owner.

To obtain permission(s) to use material from this work, please submit a written request to Allyn and Bacon, Permissions Department, 75 Arlington Street, Boston, MA 02116 or fax your request to 617-848-7320.

Between the time Web site information is gathered and then published, it is not unusual for some sites to have closed. Also, the transcription of URLs can result in typographical errors. The publisher would appreciate notification where these errors occur so that they may be corrected in subsequent editions.

Library of Congress Cataloging-in-Publication Data

Boyd-Batstone, Paul.
    Differentiated early literacy for English language learners : practical strategies / by Paul Boyd-Batstone.
      p.   cm.
    ISBN 0-205-41806-6
     1. English language—Study and teaching (Elementary)—Foreign speakers.   2. English language—Study and teaching (Elementary)—United States.   I. Title.

PE1128.A2B65 2006
28.0071'2—dc24   2005053530

Printed in the United States of America

10 9 8 7 6 5 4 3 2 1   09 08 07 06 05

Contents

7 *Teaching Writing Across Proficiency Levels   93*

PREFACE

The idea for the book, *Differentiated Early Literacy for English Language Learners: Practical Strategies,* grew out of my extensive experience working with elementary school aged English language learners (ELL) in urban classroom settings. The ELLs came from all parts of the world; from Mexico, Central and South America to China and Southeast Asia. The title of the book is comprised of four essential components. Those components are as follows: differentiated instruction, early literacy development, teaching students who are learning English as a second or additional language (ELL), and practical strategies organized according to levels of language proficiency.

The underlying premise of this book is that skilled teachers respond to the diverse strengths and needs of their students. This recognizes that teachers are the ultimate decision makers with regard to daily instruction. They are the ones that work the closest with their students. Consequently, they make the key instructional choices to match strategies and activities to those students. Therefore, skilled teachers practice differentiated instruction. They know that "one-size-does-not-fit-all." This is especially true for literacy development for ELLs who enter classrooms with a wide range of levels of proficiency in English.

Who Is the Book For?

The book was written with two types of readers in mind: pre-service and in-service teachers of ELLs. The focus of the book is on practical application of instructional strategies. Pre-service teachers will find broad categories of early literacy development accessible with an array of practical strategies matched to levels of proficiency. The strategies are easily applied to instruction with minimum preparation. Pre-service teachers will also find that the book demystifies instruction related to ELLs with plain language about how to teach to a student's language level.

In-service, or experienced, teachers will find the collection of strategies matched to levels of language proficiency, but also matched to National TESOL Standards. Matching the strategies to standards ensures that ELLs are getting comprehensive, standards-based instruction, thereby meeting the demands of "No Child Left Behind." Further, in-service teachers will find parent involvement tips throughout the book with many ways to foster and increase parent participation even though the parents may not be proficient in English or literate in their home language.

Organization of the Book

The book is organized around broad categories related to early literacy with ELLs. Chapter One introduces the connection between differentiated early literacy and ELLs in a standards-based instructional setting. TESOL National Standards are referenced and applied to each chapter of the book. Chapter two details how to quickly identify a student's level of language proficiency and how to match instruction to the appropriate level. Chapters three through seven provide standards-based strategies that are matched to levels of language proficiency. The strategies in chapter three are related to developing listening and speaking. Chapter four deals with mechanics in writing such as handwriting, grammar, and spelling. Chapter five gives a wide range of strategies for vocabulary development. Chapter six provides a selection of strategies to support reading instruction. Chapter seven includes writing across proficiency levels and supplies rubrics specific to genre and language level.

Acknowledgments

Writing a book is an organic process. It grows out of the accumulation of study, experiences, and relationships over a period of years. Foundationally, I am deeply indebted to the work of Louise Rosenblatt whose clear thinking from the 1930s continues to be influential in the present. One of my fondest memories was being invited to attend her 90th birthday party during an International Reading Association Convention in Orlando, Florida. She saw how her work on literary theory applied to issues of language and culture.

I would like to express my appreciation to Aurora Martínez, Senior Editor at Allyn and Bacon, and her capable staff for patiently working with me as the book came into its current form. Thank-you to the reviewers: Maria Dantas-Whitney, Western Oregon University; Sally Gearhart, Santa Rosa Junior College; Barbara Hruska, University of Tampa; and Diane Lapp, San Diego State University.

Much of my own understanding of teaching English language learners has been honed by working with friends and colleagues like Ron and Leslie Reese, Shelly Speigel-Coleman, Outey Khuon, and Juli Kendall. I would like to give special acknowledgment to the good people of the Guatemalan Reading Council and especially Marcie and Jerry Mondschein who have contributed so much to schools in that beautiful country. Carole Cox has been more than a mentor to me in the development of my own career. I have learned to pay very close attention to her counsel. She has never steered me in the wrong direction. Of course, I am deeply grateful to my wife, Nancy, and daughter, Kathryn, who have encouraged me to write and created space at home for me to do so.

Finally, I wish to give special acknowledgment to an inspirational friend, Mory Ouk, who died from a brain tumor this past year. Mory, a school principal in Phnom Penh, Cambodia, escaped the Khmer Rouge killing fields by sheer smarts and guile. While in a refugee camp in Thailand, he started a school for the children in the camp. Two days after immigrating to the United States, he was hired to conduct language screening for Khmer-speaking children in the Long Beach Unified School District. He was instrumental in initiating the first Khmer/English bilingual program in the United States. I had the privilege of working with him on that project. Even though his transcripts and credentials were lost in Cambodia, he became a significant resource throughout the nation for educating children from Southeast Asia. He later recovered his transcripts and became one of my students as he earned a teaching credential and a Master's Degree in Education. He taught third grade during the day, lectured at California State University, Long Beach at night, and presented at conferences all over the country. He taught me never to underestimate the value of another human being, no matter what language they speak or their country of origin. He lived to see the birth of his son "Little Mo." This book would not have been written without his inspiration. Thank you, Mory.

1

Differentiated Early Literacy for English Language Learners

Introduction

Imagine a typical elementary school classroom in an urban setting in the United States. Chances are there are a significant number of English Language Learners (ELLs) in the classroom. Current federal estimates indicate five to six million ELLs in public schools (No Child Left Behind, 2002). Yet one student may be a new arrival with little knowledge of the English language. Another student might have arrived six months earlier and is beginning to respond to open-ended questions. Another ELL might write fluently with many errors in English. And another might be mistaken for a native speaker except when discussing new topics. Each one of these students may be classified as an ELL, yet their instructional needs are diverse.

Early literacy at elementary grades for English Language Learners is a significant focus of No Child Left Behind (NCLB). The broad purpose of the legislation stated in the text of the law is to "... ensure that all children have a fair, equal, and significant opportunity to obtain a high-quality education and reach, at a minimum, proficiency on challenging State academic achievement standards ..." (No Child Left Behind, 2002). Use of national and state standards dictate a degree of uniformity of instruction; ELLs, however, are not a uniform group. They are from unique cultural, linguistic, and socioeconomic backgrounds, are of all ages and grade levels, and are placed in classrooms based on a variety of proficiency levels in English. Furthermore, much of the NCLB discussion about early literacy is defined by the following five components of reading instruction: phonemic awareness, phonics, vocabulary development, fluency, and comprehension. This book, however, is not a reading text. Differentiated instruction in early literacy for English Language Learners is the focus. Even though there is some overlap with the five reading components, the purpose of this book is to address a differentiated perspective of language arts in literacy development with the prospective and practicing teacher in mind. The book is designed to meet the demands of NCLB and to reference national Teachers of English to Speakers of Other Languages (TESOL) standards, while providing instructional strategies and activities that match levels of language proficiency.

English Language Learners and Standards

Snow (2000) advocated the use of English as a Second Language (ESL) standards to help teachers implement effective instructional practice for English Language Learners. Hakuta (2001) argued that academic standards designed for ELLs contributed to accurately evaluating academic progress, particularly in the ELLs' initial years of schooling. Others have described ways to implement ESL standards in classroom practice (Herrell & Jordan, 2004; Agor, 2000; Irujo, 2000; Samway 2000; Smallwood, 2000).

At first glance, referring to standards and differentiation in the same sentence might appear to be an oxymoron. But standards provide a framework on which to create differentiated instruction. I like the image of an Olympic diver using the structure of a diving board to launch herself into a spectacular series of twists and flips to execute the perfect dive. It is the structure underneath that supports the unique creative effort of the diver. In much the same way, the standards form the structure underneath. They do not dictate specific instructional tasks, which may vary infinitely, but they inform and support instructional decisions.

Lachat (1998) documented several benefits to using standards to inform instructional practice for ELLs. He noted that standards reverse the tendency to provide less challenging curriculum for ELLs, that standards fostered higher expectations particularly when they matched instructional practice to the process of acquiring a second language. The development of standards for ESL instruction was initially undertaken by the Teachers of English to Speakers of Other Languages (TESOL, 1997), a professional organization that established standards around three fundamental goals: 1) to use English to communicate in social settings, 2) to use English to achieve academically in all content areas, and 3) to use English in socially and culturally appropriate ways. A total of nine standards (see below), three assigned to each goal, attempt to inform all aspects of learning another language. TESOL standards provide valuable insight into ESL instruction. As the TESOL standards are virtually the only nationally accepted standards for ELLs at this time, they will be referenced throughout this book.

Even though TESOL standards are embraced on a national level, they do pose some implementation problems for elementary school teachers of ELLs. The broad categories and organization of the TESOL standards can be unspecific and insufficient to inform current NCLB instructional priorities. TESOL standards, for instance, do not differentiate between levels of language proficiency. There is no distinction between a beginning or an advanced ELL. The assumption is that the instructional needs of all ELLs are uniform, like using a one-size-fits-all approach to teaching. Examples of a uniform approach to teaching ELLs with early literacy can be found in Tomkins (1997). Conversely, the English Language Development (ELD) content standards (1999), compiled at the state level in California, applied five levels of proficiency, three basic levels and two sub-levels using the term "early": beginning, early intermediate, intermediate, early advanced, and advanced. This differentiated approach to standards fosters greater accuracy in assessment and encourages differentiated instruction for ELLs.

TESOL standards do have indicators for pre-K to third grade and fourth to eighth grade levels, but the organization of the standards is not mirrored in the early literacy priority set forth by NCLB and the National Reading Panel (2000). Early literacy is a prominent area of focus that frames instructional design in elementary school classrooms for both English-only speakers and ELLs. For example, August (2002) found that oral English proficiency is predictive of early reading success. This finding has also been linked to ELLs (Baker & Gersten, 1997; Garcia, 2000; Gersten & Geva, 2003). Therefore, elementary school classrooms tend to be structured around early literacy programs. TESOL Goal 1, however, addresses communicative competence in a variety of social settings. Social settings for children tend to be pretty narrow, so creating a variety of social settings in which to practice English is much more in line with secondary- or adult-level ESL instruction. Further, although TESOL Goal 2 addresses academic areas, three standards are insufficient to guide listening, speaking, understanding, reading, and writing in all their forms.

True, TESOL standards are beneficial for instruction and assessment of ELLs, but as argued above, they also pose certain problems for the diverse elementary school classroom. The solution, then, is to utilize and reference the informed ESL perspective of the nationally accepted

TESOL standards. However, the difference is to maintain an early literacy focus with an eye to differentiating strategies and activities across levels of English proficiency. In this book, prospective and practicing elementary school teachers of ELLs will find practical ways to teach across levels of proficiency. Key areas include standards-based strategies and activities for early literacy that are differentiated to the appropriate levels of English proficiency, a range of assessment tools to document academic progress, and ideas for increased parental involvement in keeping with the demands of No Child Left Behind.

Tips for Increasing Parental Involvement

Throughout the book the reader will find tips for involving parents. According to Purcell-Gates (2000), family literacy was identified as foundational for learning. Additionally, programs that targeted specific literacy strategies for parents were found to be effective in improving academic achievement. Literacy development areas in which parents can help their children include vocabulary development, reading fluency, and process writing.

Vocabulary instruction is key to English language development and has a significant impact on achievement in reading and writing skills (Blanchowicz & Fisher, 2000). Parents, even though they are limited English speakers themselves, can assist in vocabulary development on two levels. The first is in providing primary language (L1) support. Berndhart and Kamil (1995) documented that language development in L1 contributed to and supported language development in L2. Another way that parents assist vocabulary development is by facilitating reading at home. Considering that some parents may be illiterate or minimally literate, facilitating reading at home may require creative alternatives to directly reading to their children. Alternative ways to provide support at home may include taking children to the public library, utilizing audio-recorded books, sitting with the children as they read and asking strategic questions about the reading, and listening for fluency as their children read aloud. Specific tasks that foster language development at home are detailed throughout the book.

Strategies and Activities That Fit

The use of strategies is universal. In every facet of life, we employ a broad array of strategies. Whether it is fixing a car, cooking a meal, playing a sport, or teaching English Language Learners, each arena of life requires strategies to solve problems. Applying strategies that fit, though, requires being responsive to the complex needs at hand. Research on the use of strategies by ELLs (Chamot, Barnhardt, El-Dinary, & Robbins, 1999; Gu, Hu, & Zhang 2003) suggests that academically successful ELLs not only orchestrate a wide range of learning strategies, but they also monitor and select which ones are most useful for a given situation.

Literacy development with ELLs poses multiple situations for using strategies. The instructional needs of ELLs are as diverse as the languages they speak at home, the literacy levels they have attained, and the sociocultural backgrounds they bring to the classroom. Addressing linguistic needs requires differentiating instruction to match levels of proficiency. It also requires strategies that are situational (Lave & Wenger, 1991), and that provide ELLs with the means to explore their own identities (Toohey, 2000) and to utilize expressions of their own culturally grounded knowledge (Moll, Amanti, & Gonzalez, 1992).

Think about teaching the writing process to a group of fourth-grade ELLs. One student may be a new arrival with little education in his own language, another may come from a language group that uses non-Western script, and still another may be quite literate in her own language with a high level of proficiency in English. Certainly, an insightful teacher would not presume to teach each student in the same way. The teaching strategies used must fit the child. Matching strategies that fit the needs of the child is essentially response-oriented instruction with a focus on the ELL.

The strategies in this book are designed to respond to the ELL's level of proficiency and personal perspective. Rosenblatt (1938/1986; 1978), the seminal theorist for response-oriented pedagogy, advanced the idea of exploration of aesthetic experiences in the language arts. Bahktin (1981) argued that words by themselves are lifeless, but that languages come alive when they are uttered in the context of one's experience. On a predominantly linguistic level, the strategies and activities in this book are designed to match levels of proficiency in English. Yet, on a more global level, the strategies are also designed to address the situational interests and needs of ELLs. The selected strategies and activities invite exploration of one's experience and expression of one's knowledge while learning English.

How to Use This Book

This book works best as a reference guide rather than as a text one would read cover to cover. Book chapters address areas of early literacy development with strategies and activities arranged according to levels of proficiency. Levels of proficiency are divided into three basic groupings: beginning, intermediate, and advanced. In cases that require a finer degree of differentiation, additional levels of early intermediate and early advanced are used. These distinctions help the teacher decide which strategies would best apply to a given ELL.

The following chapters address a variety of aspects of the language arts: identification of levels of proficiency, questioning strategies, vocabulary development strategies, reading strategies, writing strategies, and the mechanics of handwriting, grammar, and spelling. This is by no means a comprehensive listing of all available strategies and activities. The selected strategies and activities were included because of their high degree of success with ELLs in the context of the classroom, and because they are easily implemented with a minimum of preparation and/or materials development.

A brief overview of the book is as follows. In Chapter two, identification of levels of proficiency does not presume to replace the complex normative measures of English language development. Nevertheless, teachers need a way to quickly assess a student's level of proficiency. Often a student arrives in a classroom with little to no background information. It may take weeks for the assessment data to be made available. Using a simple quick assessment tool, the teacher can begin to provide instruction that is appropriate for the ELL's level of proficiency. Beyond the quick assessment tool are more in-depth descriptors for each level of proficiency according to listening, speaking, reading, and writing domains of language arts. The TESOL standards are adapted to create a summative assessment with a differentiated perspective as well. The chapter finishes with a sample profile of an ELL with matching strategies to address strengths and needs.

In Chapter three, questioning strategies address oral language development. Students' oral responses can range from silent gestures to wordy narratives depending on their levels of proficiency. Included in the chapter are a number of ways to use appropriate questions and also to frame response opportunities.

In Chapter four, the mechanics of writing—specifically handwriting, grammar, and spelling—are addressed. A unique feature is the use of total physical response for each letter of the alphabet, upper and lower case, to teach handwriting. Selected grammar teaching strategies are provided. The spelling strategies draw on stages of developmental spelling and ELD techniques. Additionally, the chapter describes ten of the most baffling spelling rules that ELLs experience.

In Chapter five, vocabulary development is discussed as a key to language learning. ELLs do not perceive words the same way that literate adults do. Literate adults tend to see words as inherently meaningful. The reality is that words in isolation are abstract representations of meaning. Teaching vocabulary at a more concrete level is key to making words meaningful.

In Chapter six, reading is taught explicitly and implicitly. Since there are numerous texts on reading which address phonemic awareness and phonics, this chapter addresses reading in the long run as a way of organizing instruction in the classroom that provides explicit instruction, but structures time for independent reading that fosters a rhythm of lifelong reading. The strategies are selected to allow students to formulate their own interpretations and to explore their ideas as they read.

In Chapter seven, process-writing instruction is differentiated to accommodate the needs of specific ELLs. The strategies are selected to teach the entire writing process no matter the level of proficiency. The intention is to equip the ELL with the tools to write to a variety of genres. Included in the chapter are genre-specific rubrics for each level of student.

Matching instruction to the child with a differentiated approach is the surest way to meet broad legislative reforms. Margaret Taylor Stewart (2004) reminds us that, in light of sweeping national reforms of NCLB, it is still the classroom teacher that makes the difference. "Whatever else is mandated, teachers must create time in classrooms to attend to the needs of individual learners. Knowledgeable, caring teachers are key to implementing NCLB in ways that help children experience learning success and become lifelong learners who choose to read and write in their daily lives" (p. 740). This applies to teachers of all learners, but particularly to those prospective and practicing teachers working to meet the diverse needs of ELLs.

Appendix: TESOL Goals and Standards (1997)

Goal 1: To use English to communicate in social settings

Standard 1: Students will use English to participate in social interactions

Standard 2: Students will interact in, through, and with spoken and written English for personal expression and enjoyment

Standard 3: Students will use learning strategies to extend their communicative competence

Goal 2: To use English to achieve academically in all content areas

Standard 1: Students will use English to interact in the classroom

Standard 2: Students will use English to obtain, process, construct, and provide subject matter information in spoken and written form

Standard 3: Students will use appropriate learning strategies to construct and apply academic knowledge

Goal 3: To use English in socially and culturally appropriate ways

Standard 1: Students will use the appropriate language variety, register, and genre according to audience, purpose, and setting

Standard 2: Students will use nonverbal communication appropriate to audience, purpose, and setting

Standard 3: Students will use appropriate learning strategies to extend their sociolinguistic and sociocultural competence

References

Agor, B. (Ed.) (2000). *Integrating the ESL standards into classroom practice: Grades 9–12.* Alexandria, VA: TESOL.

August, D. (2002). *English as a second language instruction: Best practices to support the development of literacy for English language learners.* Baltimore: Johns Hopkins University, Center for Research on the Education of Students Placed at Risk.

Bahktin, M. M. (1981). The dialogic imagination. Austin, TX: University of Texas Press.

Baker, S., & Gersten, R. (1997). *Exploratory meta-analysis of instructional practices for English language learners.* (Tech Rep. No. 97-01). Eugene, OR: Eugene Research Institute.

Bernhardt, E. B., & Kamil, M. L. (1995). Interpreting relationships between L1 and L2 reading: Consolidating the linguistic threshold and the linguistic interdependence hypotheses. *Applied Linguistics*, 16, 15–34.

Blanchowicz, C., & Fisher, P. (2000). *Vocabulary instruction.* In M. L. Kamil, P. B. Mosenthal, P. D. Pearson, & R. Barr (Eds), *Handbook of reading research,* Vol III (pp. 503–523). Mahwah, NJ: Erlbaum.

California Department of Education. (1999). *English-Language Development Standards for California Public Schools.* Sacramento, CA: California Department of Education.

Chamot, A. U., Barnhardt, S., El-Dinary, P. B., & Robbins, J. (1999). *The learning strategies handbook.* White Plains, NY: Longman.

Garcia, G. (2000). Bilingual children's reading. In M. L. Kamil, P. B. Mosenthal, P. D. Pearson, & R. Barr (Eds.), *Handbook of reading research,* Vol. III (pp. 813–834). Mahwah, NJ: Erlbaum.

Gersten, R., & Geva, E. (2003). Teaching reading to early language learners. *Educational Leadership, 60* (8), 44–49.

Gu, Y., Hu, G., & Zhang, L. J. (2003). *Eliciting learning strategies from lower primary school students in Singapore.* Paper presented at the ERAS Conference, Singapore.

Hakuta, K. (2001). *The education of language minority students.* Testimony to the U.S. Commission on Civil Rights, April 13, 2001 [online]. Available: www.stanford.edu/~hakuta/Docs/Civil-RightsCommission.htm

Herrell, A., & Jordan, M. (2004). *Fifty strategies for teaching English language learners.* (2nd ed.) Upper Saddle River, NJ: Merrill/Prentice Hall.

Irujo, S. (Ed.) (2000). *Integrating the ESL standards into classroom practice: Grades 6–8.* Alexandria, VA: TESOL.

Lachat, M. A. (1998). *Shifting to standards-based learning. What does it mean for schools, teachers, and students? Educating linguistically and culturally diverse students: An ASCD professional inquiry kit.* Alexandria, VA: Association for Supervision and Curriculum Development.

Lave, J., & Wenger, E. (1991). *Situated learning: Legitimate peripheral participation.* Cambridge, England: Cambridge University Press.

Moll, L. C., Amanti, C., & Gonzalez, N. (1992). Funds of knowledge for teaching: Using a qualitative approach to connect homes and classrooms. *Theory Into Practice, 31*(2), 132–141.

National Reading Panel. (2000). *Teaching children to read: An evidence-based assessment of the scientific research literature on reading and its implications for reading instruction.* Rockville, MD: National Institute of Child Health and Human Development.

No Child Left Behind Act of 2001, Pub. L. No. 107-110, 1001, 115 Stat. 1439. (2002). Retrieved May 29, 2002 from http://edworkforce.house.gov/issues/107th/education/nclb/nclb.htm.

Purcell-Gates, V. (2000). *Family literacy.* In M. L. Kamil, P. B. Mosenthal, P. D. Pearson, & R. Barr (Eds), *Handbook of reading research,* Vol. III (pp. 853–870). Mahwah, NJ: Erlbaum.

Rosenblatt, L. (1938/1986). *Literature as exploration.* New York: MLA.

Rosenblatt, L. (1978). *The reader, the text, the poem.* Carbondale and Edwardsville, IL: Southern Illinois University Press.

Samway, K. (Ed.) (2000). *Integrating the ESL standards into classroom practice: Grades 3–5.* Alexandria, VA: TESOL.

Smallwood, B. (Ed.) (2000). *Integrating the ESL standards into classroom practice: Grades pre-K–2.* Alexandria, VA: TESOL.

Snow, M. (Ed.) (2000). *Implementing the ESL standards for pre-K–12 students through teacher education.* Alexandria, VA: TESOL.

Stewart, M. T. (May 2004). Early literacy instruction in the climate of No Child Left Behind. *Reading Teacher, 57*(8), 732–743.

TESOL (1997). *ESL standards for pre-K–12 students.* Alexandria, VA: TESOL.

Tomkins, G. E. (1997). *Literacy for the twenty-first century: A balanced approach.* Upper Saddle River, NJ: Merrill/Prentice Hall.

Toohey, K. (2000). *Learning English at school: Identity, social relations, and classroom practice.* Clevedon, England: Multilingual Matters.

2

Identifying Proficiency Levels

Matching Instructional Strategies and Student Activities

Differentiated instruction assumes that one size does *not* fit all. Prior to selecting appropriate English Language Development (ELD) strategies and activities, it is vital to identify the level of language proficiency the student has achieved in order to provide matching instructional strategies. In this chapter, assessment tools for identification of an English Language Learner's proficiency level are presented. The tools are as follows: 1) Quick Assessment of ELD Levels of Proficiency for initial identification of language level, 2) ELD Behavioral Indicators across reading/language arts domains, and 3) a reference table for teacher strategies and student activities across reading/language arts domains.

There are formal means for assessing levels of proficiency. The assessment process, however, is time consuming and requires a specialized examiner to administer a test, and in many cases there is a delay of several months between taking the initial assessment and receiving the results. Nevertheless, the teacher must begin instruction as soon as the ELL enters the classroom. The teacher needs a quick assessment of proficiency levels based upon characteristic behaviors for each level and a ready reference for which strategies and activities would be appropriate for instruction.

The TESOL standards (1997) inform assessment, yet they do not differentiate levels of English language proficiency. The way to deal with this situation is to borrow the structure from the English Language Development Standards (1999), which are divided into five basic levels of proficiency: beginning, early intermediate, intermediate, early advanced, and advanced. Each level is numbered as a stage from 1 to 5, with 1 corresponding to beginning and 5 corresponding to advanced.

The Key to Differentiated ELD

Herein lies the key to differentiated English Language Development. One set of strategies does not meet the needs of all ELLs. Identifying the appropriate level of proficiency generates a range of specific strategies and activities.

There are a number of "universal" behaviors, however, that can be attributed to ELLs at various stages of proficiency. Knowing these allows the teacher to quickly provide a rough

TABLE 2.1   *Quick Assessment of ELD Levels of Proficiency*

Level	Stage	Duration	Student Behaviors
1	Beginning	<6 months	• May remain silent/active listening • Uses gestures to convey a message • Yes/No responses predominantly • Gives 1- to 2-word expressions • Follows oral directions when modeled
2	Early Intermediate	3 months to 1 year	• Speaks simple sentences (limited to simple present and past tense) • Responds to an open-ended question • Retells events (from personal experience or in stories) • Reads basic vocabulary • May read simple sentences • Frequent grammatical errors in speech (confuses he/she, him/her; infrequent use of irregular verbs)
3	Intermediate	2 to 3 years	• Retells events using descriptive vocabulary • Summarizes narrative accounts • Identifies main ideas • Provides details orally • Makes comparisons • Identifies and defines new vocabulary orally • Relies on illustrations for reading context clues • Writes simple sentences using high-frequency words
4	Early Advanced	3 to 4 years	• Appears to be orally fluent • Begins to use discipline-specific, academic terminology (e.g., math: numerator/denominator) • Near grade level proficiency in academic areas • Comprehends grade level texts with assistance • Writes fluently with spelling and grammatical errors
5	Advanced	>3 years	• Paraphrases/synthesizes content material • Generates discussions • Socially comfortable • Understands and makes plays on words • Reads/writes at grade level

assessment in order to accommodate instruction appropriately. I have developed a quick reference (see Table 2.1). To use this quick assessment, observe the student as he participates in classroom activities, and compare the behaviors listed in the table with the kinds of behaviors the student exhibits. I have also developed a summative tool, discussed later in this chapter, that can be used to evaluate levels of language proficiency based on the descriptors for each TESOL standard and the five levels of proficiency.

Several factors come into play when assessing language levels. First of all, one must ask, is the ELL literate in his/her native language? Initial literacy assumes phonemic awareness, knowledge of concepts about print, and decoding skills. If the ELL is not literate in the primary language, then those areas must be taught. If the ELL is literate in the primary language, then grade level considerations come into play.

> ***Tip for parent involvement:*** Parents are stakeholders in the assessment process. Include them in assessment by taking time to describe levels of proficiency and expected ELL behaviors for each level. Verify your assessment with their insights into how their child uses language at home.

Levels of Proficiency

Level	Stage	Duration	Student Behaviors
1	Beginning	<6 months	• May remain silent/active listening • Uses gestures to convey a message • Gives Yes/No responses predominantly • 1- to 2-word expressions • Follows oral directions when modeled

Level 1, the Beginning Stage

When considering working with a beginning level student, I think of a traveler who is feeling lost in another country. The traveler intently looks for signs that can give direction, and makes one- to two-word utterances coupled with gestures to indicate meaning. Similarly, beginning students are easily identifiable due to their absence of a working vocabulary in English. Attempting to force a student to speak at this stage is futile and can lead to frustration for both the student and the teacher. Teachers can expect an ELL to be at this stage for a few weeks to as long as six months. Characteristic behaviors include staying silent, while actively listening for something that makes sense. A student at this level will use and respond to gestures to convey meaning. (One of the first gestures I teach beginning students is a hand sign for the bathroom.) A common behavior of nodding the head in the affirmative or shaking it to say "no" gives insight into how a teacher can communicate with a beginning student.

Key strategies. Teachers should frame Yes/No questions and model meaningful gestures to facilitate communication. Beginning students follow oral directions, such as "sit" "stand," or "raise your hand," particularly if they are modeled by the teacher or another student. (See Total Physical Response in Chapter 4.) Extensive use of visuals, models, and real objects to make communication meaningful is strongly encouraged.

Level	Stage	Duration	Student Behaviors
2	Early Intermediate	3 months to 1 year	• Speaks simple sentences (limited to simple present and past tense) • Responds to an open-ended question • Retells events (from personal experience or in stories) • Reads basic vocabulary • May read simple sentences • Frequent grammatical errors in speech (confuses he/she, him/her; infrequent use of irregular verbs)

Level 2, the Early Intermediate Stage

As a teacher, I always knew when a student moved from level 1 to level 2 by "The Tattletale Test." The moment the beginning student would come running up to me at recess and begin to tattle on another student, I would say, "Congratulations! You've achieved early intermediate fluency." Achieving this level of proficiency can take as little as three months or in some cases up to a year. In my experience, the cases that took up to a year were due in large part to lack of literacy in the home or emotional trauma related to refugee circumstances. In a caring social environment, however, it is amazing how quickly an ELL moves to early intermediate fluency.

Students at this stage begin to speak in complete, yet simple, sentences. Beginning students tell about their own experiences, and consequently, are able to retell events in order from a story that has been read to them. They can respond orally to open-ended questions such as, "What are you doing?" or "How do you feel?" Early intermediate students begin to read simple, predictable books with vivid illustrations. They can recognize key vocabulary in a sentence. They also commonly misapply gender with nouns, pronouns, and titles (he/she, him/her, Mr./Mrs.). Irregular verbs are problematic in cases such as "She *brang* (brought) it to school."

Key strategies. These behaviors invite a variety of instructional strategies including those already mentioned for Level 1. Valuable strategies for classroom teachers with students at this stage include collaborative chart stories (see Chapter 6), selecting books with vivid illustrations to enhance meaning, and providing simple books with predictable sentence patterns (see Chapter 5). Interactive journal writing allows the teacher to label student drawings and model writing using the student's own words (see Chapter 6). Another efficient teaching strategy is direct instruction of key vocabulary in stories and content area lessons (see Chapter 4).

Level	*Stage*	*Duration*	*Student Behaviors*
3	Intermediate	2 to 3 years	• Retells events using descriptive vocabulary • Summarizes narrative accounts • Identifies main ideas • Provides details orally • Makes comparisons • Identifies and defines new vocabulary orally • Relies on illustrations for reading context clues • Writes simple sentences using high-frequency words

Level 3, the Intermediate Stage

When I hear a student describe a story character with words like "delighted" or "nasty," rather than the ubiquitous "happy/sad" descriptors, I see them achieving the intermediate stage. Beyond using simple vocabulary and just retelling events, intermediate-stage students use richer vocabulary and expand on their thinking. Students at this level of proficiency begin to use language to apply higher-order thinking skills to learning. They will summarize events and main ideas. They will make comparisons to other stories or prior experiences, and will actively inquire about words they don't know and pursue definitions. When reading they look to story illustrations to provide context clues. Their writing may appear to be fluent, but upon review, high-frequency words are used extensively. Because students at this stage are working to deepen their proficiency with language, it takes time to advance to the next level, as much as two to three years.

Key strategies. The kinds of strategies that benefit an intermediate student include creating illustrated thesauruses to expand vocabulary, word study of etymologies, and use of cognates (see Chapter 4); teaching study skills like note taking, double-entry journals for citing important story parts and reflecting on the meaning, and using picture walks prior to reading (see Chapter 5); using graphic organizers to facilitate organizing ideas, exploring figurative language and employing process writing to expand simple sentences, and facilitating writing with presentation software that utilizes hypermedia (see Chapter 6).

Level	Stage	Duration	Student Behaviors
4	Early Advanced	3 to 4 years	• Appears to be orally fluent • Begins to use discipline-specific, academic terminology (e.g., math: numerator/denominator) • Near grade level proficiency in academic areas • Comprehends grade level texts with assistance • Writes fluently with spelling and grammatical errors

Level 4, the Early Advanced Stage

Students often appear to languish in intermediate and early advanced stages due to the time it actually takes to develop a deep understanding of and fluency in English. In some cases it can take as long as four years to advance to the next level. Students who are readers and writers move forward in a predictable amount of time, but those who struggle with literacy progress at much slower rates. At these levels, the differences are not readily apparent. Just listening for oral language usage is insufficient. What distinguishes each level is literacy in subject matter instruction at appropriate grade levels of complexity. A practical indicator that a student has achieved early advanced proficiency is when the student argues about a concept in a subject area using subject-specific terminology with specific references to a text. It requires literacy as well as fluency to correctly state a case and substantiate one's ideas with textual references.

Characteristic behaviors unique to the early advanced stage include oral fluency in English with few spoken grammatical errors and near grade level proficiency in academic areas. Students at this level readily learn and use terminology specific to various academic disciplines. They write with a high degree of fluency, but commonly make errors of spelling and grammar.

Key strategies. Appropriate strategies for students at this level include using comic strips or a "joke of the day" to give students the opportunity to explore wordplay with humor—when students laugh, you know they understood the language. Direct instruction of formulating questions of who, what, where, and why addresses oral ways to seek answers. Students at this level need content area vocabulary development and assistance with reading grade level textbooks. Grouping strategies with reading material that is divided up in a "jigsaw" format is helpful. Note-taking and prewriting skills are essential at this stage to aid recording and organizing thoughts in content areas.

Level	Stage	Duration	Student Behaviors
5	Advanced	>3 years	• Paraphrases/synthesizes content material • Generates discussions • Socially comfortable • Understands and makes plays on words • Reads/writes at grade level

Level 5, the Advanced Stage

What sometimes causes confusion is the assumption that the behaviors of a student at the advanced stage are essentially the same as those of a native speaker. An advanced student may still have gaps in specialized areas. For example, a student may struggle in explaining to the school nurse the exact location of physical discomfort. Or the student might feel out of place in certain culturally embedded situations such as knowing how to behave on an obscure holiday. But many of these situations can be addressed easily with a brief word of explanation because the student is so fluent in English.

A student at the advanced stage comprehends and discusses content area material with relative ease. A quick check for this stage is to ask the student to read a short selection from a grade level text and then write a brief synopsis. The ability to paraphrase and synthesize content area material distinguishes the advanced student. One should also expect the student to appear socially comfortable within a group of native speakers. A sure indicator of comfort level is to what extent the student understands a play on words. Laughter at appropriate times is a good sign of comprehension. Finally, a writing sample that demonstrates grade level proficiency is a strong indicator that the student is at an advanced level. Attaining this level may take as long as three years.

Key strategies. Fostering social interactive situations such as group projects and/or presentations addresses the social comfort level of the advanced student. Taking time to paraphrase textual material and to summarize the thoughts of another student are essential to working in content areas. Studying figurative language and plays on words in order to write limericks, joke books, and humorous stories gives the opportunity to explore nuance in the language. Advanced organizers for lectures and content reading help clarify difficult concepts.

Indicators of ELD across Language Arts Domains

The above quick assessment of levels of proficiency is a blunt tool that provides rapid identification. The following tool looks at indicators of English Language Development across the language arts domains of listening, speaking, reading, and writing (see Table 2.2). Again, by observing the student and matching indicators of English Language Development, the teacher can identify areas of strengths and needs in specific domains. Simply draw a large "X" through the box that matches the student's behaviors. This tool is followed by reference tables of teacher strategies and student activities that apply to each domain and each language level.

Reference Guide for Teacher Strategies and Student Activities

Referring to Table 2.2, imagine a student who relies on pictures to derive meaning from reading (listening/level 3), retells events from stories but does not use expanded vocabulary (speaking/level 2), reads simple picture and pattern books with some fluency (reading/level 2), and writes simple sentences using high-frequency words (writing/level 3). Recognizing those behaviors gives the teacher initial indications of strengths and needs according to language arts domains. This is the beginning of developing a personal profile for the student with recommended teacher strategies and student activities (see Table 2.8 for a sample profile).

The following is a reference section of strategies and activities appropriate for levels of proficiency of English Language Development. *Strategies* refer to what teachers do and the approaches they take for instructional purposes. *Activities* refer to what students do naturally at a given level of proficiency and what they are able to learn to do given their identified level. They are ordered according to the domains of language arts and can be used to generate instruction tailored to each ELL.

TABLE 2.2 *ELD Behavioral Indicators across Reading/Language Arts Domains*

Level/Stage	Listening	Speaking	Reading	Writing
1 **Beginning**	• May remain silent/active listening • Follows oral directions when modeled	• Uses gestures to convey a message • Yes/No responses predominantly • Gives 1- to 2-word expressions	• May have concepts about print • Follows picture books	• May write name
2 **Early Intermediate**	• Follows oral directions without modeling • Responds to an open-ended question	• Speaks simple sentences (limited to simple present and past tense) • Retells events (from personal experience or in stories) • Frequent grammatical errors in speech (confuses he/she, him/her; infrequent use of irregular verbs)	• Reads basic vocabulary • May read simple sentences • May read picture books • May read pattern books	• Copies words or simple sentences • May label items in a drawing
3 **Intermediate**	• Relies on illustrations for reading context clues • After hearing a story can recall events in order • Asks questions	• Retells events using descriptive vocabulary • Provides details orally • Makes comparisons	• Reads simple stories with illustrations • Follows written directions • Identifies and defines new vocabulary orally • Identifies main ideas • Summarizes narrative accounts	• Writes simple sentences using high-frequency words
4 **Early Advanced**	• Laughs at funny stories or jokes • Formulates what, where, how, why questions • Asks clarifying questions	• Appears to be orally fluent • Begins to use discipline-specific, academic terminology (e.g. math: numerator/denominator)	• Near grade level proficiency in academic areas • Comprehends grade level texts with assistance	• Writes fluently with spelling and grammatical errors
5 **Advanced**	• Paraphrases content material • Understands and makes plays on words • Poses higher-order questions	• Generates discussions • Socially comfortable • Formulates wordplay	• Reads at grade level	• Writes at grade level

TESOL Summative Assessment Tool

I developed the following assessment tool for the purpose of generating a summative evaluation of a student's English language proficiency according to the TESOL standards and descriptors. The assessment tool generates a quantitative measure that can be useful for making larger-scale reports of yearly progress toward advanced proficiency in English.

Goal #1, TESOL Standards and Descriptors Assessment

Scoring: 1 = Beginning (little to no communication); 2 = Early Intermediate (some communication, short phrases); 3 = Intermediate (fluent communication, frequent errors); 4 = Early Advanced (very fluent communication, some errors); 5 = Advanced (highly fluent communication, few to no errors)

Goal 1, Standard 1
To use English to communicate in social settings: Students will use English to participate in social interactions

Descriptors	1	2	3	4	5
1. Sharing and requesting information					
2. Expressing needs, feelings, and ideas					
3. Using nonverbal communication in social interactions					
4. Getting personal needs met					
5. Engaging in conversations					
6. Conducting transactions					
Subtotals					
Total					
Average Score (Total/6)					

Goal 1, Standard 2
To use English to communicate in social settings: Students will interact in, through, and with spoken and written English for personal expression and enjoyment

Descriptors	1	2	3	4	5
1. Describing, reading about, or participating in a favorite activity					
2. Sharing social and cultural traditions and values					
3. Expressing personal needs, feelings, and ideas					
4. Participating in popular cultural events					
Subtotals					
Total					
Average Score (Total/4)					

Goal 1, Standard 3

To use English to communicate in social settings: Students will use learning strategies to extend their communicative competence

Descriptors	1	2	3	4	5
1. Testing hypotheses about language					
2. Listening to and imitating how others use English					
3. Exploring alternative ways of saying things					
4. Focusing attention selectively					
5. Seeking support and feedback from others					
6. Comparing nonverbal and verbal cues					
7. Self-monitoring and self-evaluating language development					
8. Using the primary language to ask for clarification					
9. Learning and using language "chunks"					
10. Selecting different media to help understand language					
11. Practicing new language					
12. Using context to construct meaning					
Subtotals					
Total					
Average Score (Total/12)					
Standard Score (Sum of Average Scores/3)					

Note high and low extreme scores as benchmark indicators of strengths or needs.

Goal #2, TESOL Standards and Descriptors Assessment

Scoring: 1 = Beginning (little to no communication); 2 = Early Intermediate (some communication, short phrases); 3 = Intermediate (fluent communication, frequent errors); 4 = Early Advanced (very fluent communication, some errors); 5 = Advanced (highly fluent communication, few to no errors)

Goal 2, Standard 1

To use English to achieve academically in all content areas: Students will use English to interact in the classroom

Descriptors	1	2	3	4	5
1. Following oral and written directions, implicit and explicit					
2. Requesting and providing clarification					

	1	2	3	4	5
3. Participating in full class, group, and pair discussions					
4. Asking and answering questions					
5. Requesting information and assistance					
6. Negotiating and managing interactions to accomplish task					
7. Explaining actions					
8. Elaborating and extending other people's ideas and words					
9. Expressing likes, dislikes, and needs					
Subtotals					
Total					
Average Score (Total/9)					

Goal 2, Standard 2

To use English to achieve academically in all content areas: Students will use English to obtain, process, construct, and provide subject matter information in spoken and written form

Descriptors	1	2	3	4	5
1. Comparing and contrasting information					
2. Persuading, arguing, negotiating, evaluating, and justifying					
3. Listening to, speaking, reading, and writing subject matter information					
4. Gathering information orally and in writing					
5. Retelling information					
6. Selecting, connecting, and explaining information					
7. Analyzing, synthesizing, and inferring from information					
8. Responding to the work of peers and others					
9. Representing information visually and interpreting information presented visually					
10. Hypothesizing and predicting					
11. Formulating and asking questions					
12. Understanding and producing technical vocabulary and text features according to content area					
13. Demonstrating knowledge through application in a variety of contexts					
Subtotals					
Total					
Average Score (Total/13)					

Goal 2, Standard 3

To use English to achieve academically in all content areas: Students will use appropriate learning strategies to construct and apply academic knowledge

Descriptors	1	2	3	4	5
1. Focusing attention selectively					
2. Applying basic reading comprehension skills: skimming, scanning, previewing, and reviewing text					
3. Using context to construct meaning					
4. Taking notes to record important information and aid one's own learning					
5. Applying self-monitoring and self-corrective strategies to build and expand a knowledge base					
6. Determining and establishing the conditions that help one become an effective learner					
7. Planning how and when to use cognitive strategies and applying them appropriately to a learning task					
8. Actively connecting new information to information previously learned					
9. Evaluating one's own success in a completed learning task					
10. Recognizing the need for and seeking assistance appropriately from others					
11. Imitating the behaviors of native English speakers to complete tasks successfully					
12. Knowing when to use native language resources to promote understanding					
Subtotals					
Total					
Average Score (Total/12)					
Standard Score (Sum of Average Scores/3)					

Note high and low extreme scores as benchmark indicators of strengths or needs.

Goal #3, TESOL Standards and Descriptors Assessment

Scoring: 1 = Beginning (little to no communication); 2 = Early Intermediate (some communication, short phrases); 3 = Intermediate (fluent communication, frequent errors); 4 = Early Advanced (very fluent communication, some errors); 5 = Advanced (highly fluent communication, few to no errors)

Goal 3, Standard 1

To use English in socially and culturally appropriate ways: Students will use the appropriate language variety, register, and genre according to audience, purpose, and setting

Descriptors	1	2	3	4	5
1. Using the appropriate degree of formality with different audiences and settings					
2. Recognizing and using standard English and vernacular dialects appropriately					

	1	2	3	4	5
3. Using a variety of writing styles appropriate for different audiences, purposes, and settings					
4. Responding to and using slang appropriately					
5. Responding to and using idioms appropriately					
6. Responding to and using humor appropriately					
7. Determining when it is appropriate to use a language other than English					
8. Determining appropriate topics for interaction					
Subtotals					
Total					
Average Score (Total/8)					

Goal 3, Standard 2

To use English in socially and culturally appropriate ways: Students will use nonverbal communication appropriate to audience, purpose, and setting

Descriptors	1	2	3	4	5
1. Interpreting and responding appropriately to nonverbal cues and body language					
2. Demonstrating knowledge of acceptable nonverbal classroom behaviors					
3. Using acceptable tone, volume, stress, and intonation in various social settings					
4. Recognizing and adjusting behavior in response to nonverbal cues					
Subtotals					
Total					
Average Score (Total/4)					

Goal 3, Standard 3

To use English in socially and culturally appropriate ways: Students will use appropriate learning strategies to extend their sociolinguistic and sociocultural competence

Descriptors	1	2	3	4	5
1. Observing and modeling how others speak and behave in a particular situation or setting					
2. Experimenting with variations of language in social and academic settings					
3. Seeking information about appropriate language use and behavior					
4. Self-monitoring and self-evaluating language use according to setting and audience					
5. Analyzing the social context to determine appropriate language use					
6. Rehearsing variations for language in different social and academic settings					
7. Deciding when use of slang is appropriate					

	Subtotals					
	Total					
	Average Score (Total/7)					
	Standard Score (Sum of Average Scores/3)					

Note high and low extreme scores as benchmark indicators of strengths or needs.

Sample English Language Learner Profile

Utilizing Tables 2.3 through 2.7 and the Summative Assessment Tool, the teacher can quickly generate an individual profile of an English Language Learner with recommended strategies and activities for instruction. Another use of generating the profile is to group students with like strengths and needs for more efficient instruction at appropriate levels. Table 2.8 shows a sample profile that details a student's domains of strengths and needs.

TABLE 2.3   *Beginning Level*

Reading/Language Arts Domains	Teacher Strategies	Student Activities
Listening	• Provide realia and visuals, model gestures • Total Physical Response	• May remain silent/active listening • Follow oral directions when modeled
Speaking	• Do not force speech • Ask Yes/No questions • Use simple speech, caretaker speech	• Use gestures to convey a message • Yes/No responses • Make lists of items to categorize & sort
Reading	• Read to student • Show stories on video • Supply picture books • Teach letter and word recognition • Label pictures	• Listen to story • Select picture books to read • Categorize and sort letters, items, or pictures
Writing	• Model and illustrate writing on charts • Provide journals for writing and drawing	• May write name • Trace letters and simple words • Draw pictures

TABLE 2.4   *Early Intermediate Level*

Reading/Language Arts Domains	Teacher Strategies	Student Activities
Listening	• Write directions on charts • Ask students to model written directions • Provide a variety of hand signals to check for understanding	• Follows oral directions with and without modeling • Use hand signals to indicate understanding

(continued)

TABLE 2.4   (Continued)

Reading/Language Arts Domains	Teacher Strategies	Student Activities
Speaking	• Ask cloze questions • Ask open-ended questions • Conduct collaborative interviews • Tap prior knowledge and experience • Model appropriate speech • Mirror speech back to students • Provide interactive word games to develop fluency	• Give short answers • Respond to an open-ended question • Discuss story events and character traits • Compare story to prior experiences • Play interactive word games to develop fluency
Reading	• Provide buddy readers or cross-age readers • Conduct word sorting • Supply simple picture and pattern books • Choral read chart stories • Recite chart poems • Sing charted songs • Repeated reading for fluency development • Make big books • Teach vocabulary with visuals/realia/models	• Listen to cross-age readers • Read with a partner • Read picture books • Read pattern books • Match word cards to pictures • Sort word families • Practice repeated reading • Read big books • Study vocabulary
Writing	• Interactive journal writing • Encourage invented spelling • Language Experience Approach	• Copy words or simple sentences • Label items in a drawing • Participate in collaborative chart stories • Make pattern books • Make big books

TABLE 2.5   *Intermediate Level*

Reading/Language Arts Domains	Teacher Strategies	Student Activities
Listening	• Take book walks and picture walks • Teach basic story elements • Use story pictures to sequence events in order • Teach questioning • Ask students to paraphrase directions	• Preview pictures in stories • After hearing a story, recall events in order • Ask questions • Paraphrase oral directions
Speaking	• Ask cloze questions • Ask open-ended questions • Conduct collaborative interviews • Tap prior knowledge and experience • Model appropriate speech • Mirror speech back to students • Provide interactive word games to develop fluency	• Retell events using descriptive vocabulary • Make comparisons • Make and maintain a personal dictionary and thesaurus

Reading	• Teach literary analysis • Facilitate literary response • Use reference materials (dictionaries, thesaurus, encyclopedia) • Teach reading fluency • Guide discussions of reading • Teach genres	• Read simple stories with illustrations • Follow written directions • Identify and define new vocabulary orally • Identify main ideas • Summarize narrative accounts • Identify genres
Writing	• Employ double-entry journals • Teach process writing • Use graphic organizers for prewriting • Use word banks and writing frames • Encourage expanded vocabulary use • Analyze genres of writing • Use rubric assessment	• Cite and comment on important passages in double-entry journals • Prewrite using a graphic organizer • Access reference materials • Create word banks and writing frames • Differentiate narrative from informational writing • Learn/practice rubric criteria

TABLE 2.6 *Early Advanced Level*

Reading/Language Arts Domains	Teacher Strategies	Student Activities
Listening	• Tell a joke of the day • Use comic strips • Teach *Wh* questions • Call for students to formulate questions	• Respond to funny stories or jokes • Formulate what, where, how, why questions • Ask clarifying questions
Speaking	• Teach content ELD • Preview key terminology with content area instruction • Study word origins • Practice fluency development with interactive games such as charades, lingo bingo, who am I?	• Begin to use discipline-specific, academic terminology (e.g. math: numerator/denominator) • Give oral presentations • Practice fluency with word games
Reading	• Guide content reading • Jigsaw lengthy textual material • Provide advanced organizers of reading material • Read to learn information • Provide reference material	• Read grade level texts with assistance • Cooperative groups for reading • Outline informational reading • Look up key words in reference material
Writing	• Provide instruction of grammar rules • Teach spelling rules • Teach note taking • Use prewriting graphic organizers • Teach outlining	• Practice editing common grammatical errors • Write notes from lectures, videos, texts • Outline readings • Use graphic organizers for writing • Write in all genres

TABLE 2.7 *Advanced Level*

Reading/Language Arts Domains	Teacher Strategies	Student Activities
Listening	• Ask students to paraphrase • Practice wordplay • Teach higher-order questioning	• Paraphrase content material • Make plays on words • Pose higher-order questions
Speaking	• Assign leadership roles in cooperative groups • Establish a rubric for oral presentations	• Generate discussions • Organize group presentations of student work • Produce video programs
Reading	• Literature circle • Encourage personal responses to literature • Supply a wide range of books in literature and content areas	• Grade level literary analysis • Grade level literary response • Select books from all genres • Maintain individual reading log
Writing	• Teach writing multifaceted projects • Provide research tools • Provide computer technology • Teach presentation software	• Produce complex writing projects • Use word processing tools • Create multimedia presentations

TABLE 2.8 *Sample English Language Learner Profile*

Strengths	Needs
Level: 3/Listening and Writing	**Level**: 2/Speaking and Reading
Listening: relies on pictures to derive meaning from reading	**Speaking**: retells personal and events from stories but does not use expanded vocabulary
Writing: writes simple sentences using high-frequency words	**Reading**: reads simple picture and pattern books with some fluency

Recommended Instructional Strategies and Student Activities

Listening
Strategies:
• Take book walks and picture walks
• Teach basic story elements
• Use story pictures to sequence events in order
• Teach questioning
• Ask student to paraphrase directions

Activities:
• Preview pictures in stories
• After hearing a story can recall events in order

Speaking
Strategies:
• Ask cloze questions
• Ask open-ended questions
• Conduct collaborative interviews
• Tap prior knowledge and experience
• Model appropriate speech
• Mirror speech back to student
• Provide interactive word games to develop fluency

Activities:
• Give short answers
• Respond to an open-ended question

- Ask questions
- Paraphrase oral directions

- Discuss story events and character traits
- Compare story to prior experiences
- Play interactive word games to develop fluency

Writing
Strategies:
- Employ double-entry journals
- Teach process writing
- Use graphic organizers for prewriting
- Use word banks and writing frames
- Encourage expanded vocabulary use
- Analyze genres of writing
- Use rubric assessment

Activities:
- Cite and comment on important passages in double-entry journals
- Prewrite using a graphic organizer
- Access reference materials
- Create word banks and writing frames
- Differentiate narrative from informational writing
- Learn/practice rubric criteria

Reading
Strategies:
- Provide buddy readers or cross-age readers
- Conduct word sorting
- Supply simple picture and pattern books
- Choral read chart stories
- Recite chart poems
- Sing charted songs
- Repeated reading for fluency development
- Teach vocabulary with visuals/realia/models

Activities:
- Listen to cross-age readers
- Read with a partner
- Read picture books
- Read pattern books
- Match word cards to pictures
- Sort word families
- Practice repeated reading for fluency
- Read big books
- Study vocabulary

References

California Department of Education. (1999). *English-Language Development Standards for California Public Schools.* Sacramento, CA: California Department of Education.

O'Malley, J. M., & Valdez-Pierce, L. (1996). *Authentic assessment for English Language Learners: Practical approaches for teachers.* White Plains, NY: Addison Wesley Longman.

TESOL (1997). *ESL standards for pre-K–12 students.* Alexandria, VA: TESOL.

3

Strategies to Develop Listening and Speaking

TESOL Goals and Standards

GOAL 1: *To use English to communicate in social settings*

Standard 1: *Students will use English to participate in social interactions*

Standard 2: *Students will interact in, through, and with spoken and written English for personal expression and enjoyment*

Standard 3: *Students will use learning strategies to extend their communicative competence*

Listening and speaking are foundational domains of language. There are numerous ways to embed instructional strategies that target these domains. In this chapter, I will discuss accommodating teacher talk to facilitate listening and speaking; the use and management of Total Physical Response for students at early levels of fluency; facilitating student interaction with grouping strategies; the use of humor and wordplay to enhance social interaction; and questioning strategies to foster higher-order thinking, listening, and speaking.

Teacher Talk

The teacher of ELLs must employ mental discipline when speaking. Two useful strategies to accommodate teacher talk are mirroring speech and adjusting pacing.

Mirroring Speech

Mirroring speech means responding to a student's question or statement by using that student's words, but modeling the appropriate use of terminology, grammar, and syntax. This technique allows the teacher to address miscues without putting the ELL on the spot. The ELL student risks embarrassment when speaking up in class. Correcting a syntax error or an error of noun–verb agreement in front of the class may only result in silencing the student. Mirrored responses show the student conventional speech indirectly. It also establishes that the content of what the student wanted to say is important.

When mirroring speech, keep in mind the following:

- If the student employs syntax that is reflective of his/her native language, to the degree possible, use the student's choice of words, but in conventional order according to English. For example:

ELL: I see the *balloon red*.
T: A red balloon? Where do you see a red balloon?

- Avoid criticizing the language usage of the student. This is no time to risk embarrassing the student and thus silencing her attempts at speaking in front of a group of peers. There is simply no benefit to saying, "That's not how you say it. You should say . . ."
- Be prepared to negotiate the student's intended meaning. As you rephrase the student's words, ask clarifying questions such as: Did you mean . . .? or Would you say . . .?

Adjusting Pacing

In our fast-paced environment, there is a tendency to want to cover the content as quickly as possible. However, keep in mind this mantra: Speed Kills! Fast-paced speech on the part of the teacher will only lead to confusion and frustration on the part of the ELL. "Slow and steady" will enhance the comfort level of students and increase their ability to comprehend. Bill Cosby, comedian and educator, exemplified pacing. As you listen to his early comedy routines, you hear him talking extremely fast as if he is racing to pack as many jokes in as possible. As he matured, his pacing slowed and his routines became funnier and much more poignant. In much the same way, a classroom teacher must speak with intention at a slightly slower pace.

Key ways to facilitate pacing

- Plan ahead. Outline the lesson content. Be able to summarize the main points of your lesson in a few bullet statements.

- Differentiate teachable moments, mini-lessons, full lesson plans, and multiday plans.

- Stick to your agenda. Avoid getting derailed from the lesson plan. If a student brings up an interesting idea that would move the discussion elsewhere, note the insightful comment and suggest a later time to explore the issue. Pull the group back on track with a brief summary of what was discussed up to that point.

- Pause after you finish a main point. Check for understanding by asking students to paraphrase to each other what you just said.

- Learn to anticipate the clock. Good teachers have a highly developed sense of how long an activity will take. In other words, be a clock watcher.

- When asking a question, wait for students to process. Count to ten silently. (To ensure wait time, I hold my hands behind my back and physically count using my fingers while waiting for students to respond.)

- Get used to moments of silence as students ponder what you just said.

Total Physical Response: Instructional Techniques and Management Strategies

James Asher (1982) conceived of Total Physical Response (TPR) as a strategic way to teach language. In brief, TPR is modeling physical movements to convey meaning on a nonverbal level. The technique was developed originally to help patients of brain trauma recover speech, and it has found broad application with instruction for ELLs as well. TPR is especially strategic for beginners and early intermediate students.

In one case, Asher asked a Japanese teacher to demonstrated TPR with the Japanese word *kobe.* Rather than writing the definition of the word and asking students to use it in a sentence, he held hands with two students and walked three steps, counting "one, two, three." On the third step, they jumped into the air as the teacher said "kobe!" They repeated the action several times. As the students performed the action, they learned that *kobe* means "jump." It was a total physical experience of meaning.

Prior to discussing the strategy itself, a word must be said about meaning and nonverbal experiences in language development. Whether we realize it or not, meaning is predominantly nonverbal. We understand much about the world around us before we have conventional labels, or names, for objects and concepts. Think for a moment about how a baby understands "hug" and "caress" long before he knows the word or is even able to articulate the word. As adults, we can enjoy a flowering plant before we know its name. The point is what comes first. A meaningful experience precedes a name or a label for it. TPR provides meaningful, nonverbal experiences of movement and then labels the experience. The verbal experience (spoken and written words) follows the nonverbal experience.

Think of TPR as a series of commands given by the teacher, who models the action for students to perform in turn. Some have equated TPR with the popular children's game "Simon Says." Whereas with "Simon Says" you are trying to catch someone off-guard and eliminate them from the group, TPR seeks to make commands for actions comprehensible to all learners. This is not a competition; it is an effort to create a meaningful experience. A typical TPR lesson might look like the following:

Total Physical Response Lesson

Theme: Drawing a Face

Materials or props: Paper, pencils

Series of Commands:

1. You are going to draw a face.

2. Draw an oval shape for the head.

3. Make an *L* shape for the nose in the middle.

4. Trace the letter *C* on either side for ears.

5. Don't forget to flip the letter *C* on the right side.

6. Draw a small circle above the nose on either side for the eyes.

7. Scribble eyebrows over each eye.

8. Rub your finger over the eyebrows to smear the lines.

9. Spike hair on the top of the head.

10. Use a half-circle to make the mouth smile.

Target Vocabulary

Commands (Verbs)	Facial Parts (Nouns)	Shapes (Nouns)	Positions (Prepositional phrases)
draw	face	oval	in the middle
make	head	*L* shape	on either side
trace	nose	the letter *C*	on the right side
flip	ears	small circle	above
scribble	eyes	half-circle	over
rub	eyebrows		on the top
smear	hair		
spike	mouth		
use	smile		

Tip for parent involvement: Once the student learns the series of commands for a given TPR lesson, send home a one-page sheet with the TPR commands. The child can practice being the teacher and give the commands to members of the family. This will have the added effect of fostering reading.

Key points with using TPR

• Write the commands in large letters on chart paper. This gives students something to refer to and establishes basic reading skills such as concepts about print and word recognition.

• Number each command for quick reference.

• Highlight the verb in each command in a different color for easy recognition.

• Be sure to physically model the actions written on the chart paper. Simply giving commands without demonstration does not convey nonverbal meaning.

• Use a prop to help convey meaning. (For example, use a scarf to demonstrate prepositional phrases such as "wave it over your head," "hold it below your waist," and so forth.)

• Draw illustrations on the chart of the key prop as well as the actions.

• Begin a unit with a TPR lesson to help establish a theme for the instruction. Start off each day with a sequence of TPR commands.

How to conduct a TPR lesson:

1. Begin the lesson by displaying the chart of commands and showing the object(s), if any, that will be used as props.
2. Point to #1 with your finger as you read and demonstrate the command.
3. Ask all students to follow the command.
4. Point to #2 with your finger and, as above, read and demonstrate the command. (Continue with each command written on the chart.)
5. Call on volunteer students to help model the actions for the entire class.
6. Next time you teach the lesson, divide the students into small groups and assign a student to be the group leader. Have the group leader model the commands, either as the teacher reads aloud, or as a more fluent student reads aloud the commands to the class.
7. Keep the current TPR chart on display so that students can practice with a partner during a centers time or during a free time.

Assessment of TPR

Total Physical Response is a matter of student performance. Performance is appropriately assessed by using a rubric. It is possible to assess TPR with a simple rubric: 4 = Follows all commands; 3 = Follows most commands; 2 = Follows few commands; 1 = Follows no commands. A more detailed rubric format allows the teacher to assess the degree to which the student performs according to specified line items. It recognizes the qualitative difference between following, identifying, and reading the charted commands in the TPR lesson (see example below). I prefer to use a line item rubric format because it allows the teacher to differentiate areas of strength and need. The line item rubric provides a rapid way to check off ratings of the student's performance. There is also a space to include brief observational comments.

TPR Rubric Criteria	4 all	3 most	2 few	1 none	Comments
• Followed modeled commands					
• Identified key verbs by gesture and action					
• Read commands accurately					

Interpreting The Rubric

The four-point rating system permits the evaluator to readily assess attainment of the criteria. In a four-point system there is no middle ground. It forces the evaluator to decide whether or not the student met the criteria. This system makes for a clear evaluation of the student's performance. A rating of 3 or 4 would mean attaining the criteria, while a rating of 1 or 2 would mean not meeting the criteria.

The three criteria statements establish a graded level of difficulty. In other words, the first criterion statement, in terms of language usage, is easier to attain than the next. "Followed modeled commands" means conducting the action dictated by the written commands as modeled by the teacher. "Identified key verbs by gesture and action" refers to the student being able to point to the appropriate verb in a written command and do the applicable action. "Read commands accurately" refers to reading the written commands fluently from the chart.

Beginning students would be expected to follow modeled commands to a certain degree, but would not be expected to identify the key verbs in each command. Nor would they be expected to read the written commands. Early intermediate students should be able to identify key verbs and read some commands. Intermediate students should be able to attain a rating of 3 or 4 for each rubric criterion.

Grouping Strategies for Student Interaction

As a teacher educator, I observe teachers on a weekly basis. Quality teachers recognize the benefit of student-to-student interaction. Language is developed in socially interactive environments. A key strategy for facilitating social interaction is to arrange the classroom for listening and speaking purposes. Several considerations about grouping students come into play: grouping students according to language level; building flexibility into student groups; and forming questions to maximize student interaction.

Grouping Students According to Language Level

Conventional wisdom would place beginning-level students at the front of the room followed by more proficient students, with the most proficient at the back of the room. The thinking here assumes that the room is arranged in straight rows and that the teacher delivery is basically lecture/discussion mode. Since it is easier to hear in the front of the room, placing the beginner ELLs in front appears to make sense. The problem with this approach, however, is that when it comes time for students to interact, the more advanced students at the back will talk, but the less advanced students at the front will remain silent. The beginner ELLs are all grouped together and have a limited capacity to interact. In reality, they provide each other little, if any, accurate modeling for conventional English.

A much better approach would be to form heterogeneous table groups with a mixture of language levels in each table group. In the reality of the classroom, it is impractical to try to maintain a mathematically perfect balance of each language level; nevertheless, mixing students across language levels ensures that a stronger English model is within listening/speaking distance of every beginner ELL.

Grouping students for interaction means setting up table groups with an even number of students at each table for partnering. If at all possible avoid setting up a table with an odd number of students, to lessen the chance that someone will be left out.

Using Humor and Wordplay to Facilitate Social Interaction

Malcolm Douglass (1989) posed a problem regarding the assessment of comprehension. How can one really know if a listener actually understood what was said? One solution he posited was humor. If the listener laughs at a joke, one can assume that comprehension has been demonstrated. If the listener responds otherwise, one can assume that it is either a bad joke or there was no comprehension.

The premise appears to make sense; but, oh, if it were all that simple. I will never forget checking the aural comprehension of a first grader, a new arrival from El Salvador. He spoke

Spanish and a little English. He had a charming smile and enthusiasm about responding to questions. The conversation went something like this:

Me:	"I'm going to ask you something funny. Do you have three ears?"
Student:	Giggling and smiling confidently, "No."
Me:	"That's right, you know you don't have three ears. How many ears do you have?"
Student:	Again smiling confidently, "Six."

What I first imagined was having a conversation with a child with six ears; but I came to realize that the student, being six years old, was hearing the question according to Spanish syntax. In Spanish, *¿Cuántos años tienes?* literally reads, "How many *years* do you have?" He thought I was joking about his age. What the above scenario suggests is that humor can be a complex matter. Laughing at a joke does not necessarily equate to comprehension.

Tip for parent involvement: As a homework assignment, have students collect jokes from family members. Compile the jokes into a joke book that can be read at home.

There is a wonderful place for jokes and humor in learning English, though. Using jokes strategically requires matching levels of proficiency to types of jokes:

1. Beginning and early intermediate fluency: Funny scenario
2. Intermediate fluency and above: Mixing homophones
3. Intermediate fluency and above: Comic strip bubbles
4. Early advanced fluency and above: Wordplay

Funny scenario. Years ago, I was traveling in La Paz, Bolivia. I had only recently arrived there. At a local restaurant, I ordered a meal with several items. What I did not realize was the quantity of each item I ordered. When the food arrived, my solo meal was enough to feed a banquet of ten people. All I could do was laugh. Reenacting that kind of scenario has universal appeal. With very few words, an ELL can demonstrate meaningful humor. If the teacher acts as the director for the scenario by calling out a list of commands, it complements Total Physical Response. Think of the universal appeal of Punch and Judy, puppets that date back to medieval times. The humor is basically a funny scenario of two puppets and slapstick. Although I am not advocating having students perform slapstick with each other, I am suggesting that reenacting a funny scenario with puppets or people is a meaningful way to insert humor into instruction.

The following are possible scenarios to reenact:

- Ordering an item at a restaurant which turns out to be too much, or too little, or other than what was ordered
- Losing your glasses and finding them on your face
- Bumping into an acquaintance and forgetting her name
- Getting the wrong directions to school

With each of the above scenarios, the instructor is teaching questioning strategies. At the restaurant, one is playing a waiter taking orders and inquiring about each item. The other is playing the restaurant patron who is asking about the food selection. With losing your glasses, imagine one student wearing a pair of glasses and going around the room asking other students, "Have you seen my glasses?" "Where are my glasses?" While others respond with, "Have you checked your face?"

or "I don't know." In the scenario of the acquaintance, one party chitchats while the other tries to find out the name of the person without asking right out, "What is your name?" Getting lost and having to ask directions again is a repetitive way to practice asking directions.

The way one produces a funny scenario for instructional purposes is to create a script chart. A script chart is a two-column chart in large print so that all can see. In the left column are the directions to be read aloud and modeled by the instructor. In the right column are the corresponding words, phrases, or sentences that the student will be saying.

Sample Scenario: *"Getting the wrong directions to school"*
Cast: *Student, friend #1, friend #2, friend #3.*
Props: *A school sign*

Actions	*Lines*
1. Walk to the right. 2. Point to the right.	Student: "Which way to school?" Friend #1: "Walk right down this street."
3. Continue to walk to the right. 4. Point to the left.	Student: "Where is the school?" Friend #2: "Walk to the left, down this street."
5. Walk to the left. 6. Point to the right.	Student: "How do I get to school?" Friend #3: "Walk right down this street."
7. Walk to the right. Shake your head left to right. 8. Turn around.	Student: "Do you know where the school is?" Friend #4: "It's behind you."

Notice the various conceptual and language instructions the above scenario presents. First, the actions dictate directionality. Second, notice that each question asks the same thing, while providing the ELL with a repertoire of questions to use.

Mixing homophones. Mixing homophone pairs (words that sound alike, but are written differently and have different meanings) is an appropriate strategy for students at the intermediate level because it requires a level of vocabulary development prior to participation. Students must also be able to visualize the difference between paired homophones.

Prior to creating humorous pairings of homophones, students need to establish a homophone picture bank. A picture bank is created simply by folding a piece of paper in half lengthwise to make left- and right-hand sides of the paper. Write in the homophone pair, one word on each side. For example, use the word pair "hair/hare." Write "hair" on the left side of the fold and "hare" on the right side of the fold.

hair	hare

Then ask students to illustrate each word on the corresponding side. Students who do not like to draw can cut and glue magazine pictures, or utilize computer clip art. (When searching on-line for child-friendly clip art selections, I prefer to use a children's search engine like www.yahooligans.com.)

For the picture bank, collect a wide range of homophone pairs with their accompanying illustrations. Post the various illustrated pairs on a bulletin board or on a large sheet of chart paper. Display the picture bank for children to use as a quick reference for their humorous writing.

Next, select a homophone pair from the picture bank to use in a humorous way. Note how one of the words is used, and then substitute its homophone pair. For example, let's look at "hair styling." Now substitute the homophone "hare" to produce "hare styling." Imagine how a picture of "hare styling" would look. I imagine a rabbit going into a beauty parlor, or better yet, one exiting a beauty parlor with a fancy hairdo. Or should I say, "hare-do."

Begin by modeling the substitution of homophone pairs and the students will get the idea. The illustration is the key to the process. Give them time to think about combinations of images first, then follow with appropriate words. Remember that the image drives the humor; the nonverbal aspect of the meaning is the funny part of the exercise. This tells us that meaning takes place predominantly at a nonverbal level.

Comic strip bubbles. Using images to generate humorous language play is vital to making language development meaningful for ELLs. For students who are able to write in English at the intermediate level or above, filling in cartoon bubbles is an excellent exercise. This activity is ideal for a learning center activity.

Comic strip bubbles are the rounded shapes in comic strips where dialog or thoughts appear. Having students supply their own words for the pictures is an easy and meaningful way to use written language. Simply cut out your favorite comic strip from the newspaper. (Black and white comics work better for this activity.) Use liquid "white-out" to blank out the words in the bubbles. Then photocopy the comic strip with blank cartoon bubbles. You may need to enlarge the image so that there will be room to write in words. Next ask the students to fill in the comic strip bubbles with their own dialog. It is that simple. Remember that this is used strictly for educational purposes.

Several things to remember: 1) Prior to writing in the bubbles, ask the students to write and edit their words on a separate sheet of paper. This also gives the writer an indication of the space and the size of the letters to use. 2) You are appropriating published material for educational purposes only. Do not publish the work in a school newsletter, or other publication, without obtaining written permission from the publisher. 3) As a follow-up activity, students can create their own comic strips based on their own original drawings.

Wordplay. The most open-ended strategy for injecting humor into language development is wordplay; thus it is best done by more advanced ELLs. In other words, the more words students know the more they can play with. Nevertheless, all students may participate to the extent that they are able. When you want to have some fun with words, play one of the following games with your students.

Team Webbing: *A word webbing activity in a team/competitive setting.*

Purpose: To generate as many word associations as possible related to a core word in just five minutes.

Materials: Core word cards, blank paper and pencils.

Preparation: Write selected words on word cards in two-inch letters. These will be the "core words" for the game. The core words can be any words you choose. I recommend that they be words from a spelling list, or from an instructional unit in a subject area.

Directions:

1. Divide the class into teams with two students on a team.

2. Hand each team a piece of blank paper to share.

3. In the center of the paper, ask one member of each team to draw an oval large enough to accommodate a core word.

4. Show the first core word card so that all can see it.

5. Ask the second member of each team to copy the word in the oval in the center of the piece of paper.

6. At the command, "Go!", team members take turns drawing a line from the center and writing a word that is associated with the core word.

7. You may draw a line from a new word associated with the core word and write another association, thus expanding the web.

8. After five minutes, all teams stop writing.

9. Words are then counted on the webs and verified for spelling and justifiable associations.

10. The team with the most verified words on the web wins.

Rules:

1. One pencil per team.

2. Team members must take turns writing associated words. No pencil hogging.

3. All words must be spelled correctly to be included in the web.

4. Random words or words with dubious associations will not be counted.

5. Opponents can challenge words that do not appear to have a meaningful association.

6. The writer of a word being challenged must justify her word to the referee.

7. The teacher or designee acts as a referee.

8. The web with the most correctly spelled, verified words wins.

Variation of the game: Use plastic transparencies with water-soluble writing pens in lieu of paper. These are reusable, and allow the class to see a completed web all at once as it is projected on a screen using an overhead projector. This will lead to lively discussion and challenges from the class, resulting in whole class teachable moments.

Hot Words: A variation of that old familiar game, hot potato, but with words.

Purpose: To generate as many words as possible of like initial letters from a key word in a set period of time.

Materials: An egg timer, a set of word cards in the shape of a potato.

Preparation: Cut brown tagboard into potatolike shapes. Write selected words on the cards to be used in the game.

Directions:

1. Form circle groups of approximately six to eight participants.

2. Set an egg timer for three minutes.

3. Give a player in the circle a potato word card.

4. At the command, "Hot Word, Go!" the first player reads the word and then says another word with the same initial letter. (For example: If the potato word is "barrel," then the player would need to say another word beginning with *b*, such as "bitter.")

5. After successfully saying a word of like initial letter, the player passes the potato word card to any other player in the circle.

6. The next player to receive the potato word card must then state another word beginning with the same initial letter.

7. Continue passing the potato word card and generating same initial letter words.

8. When a player is unable to think of a new word—one that has not already been used—that player is out of the round.

9. Play resumes until no more words can be generated and/or one player is left.

10. Once the timer sounds, a new word is thrown into the circle and the old word is removed.

11. The round is over when only one player is left.

Rules:

1. Generated words must match the initial letter in the potato word card.

2. A player is out if he cannot think of a word with the appropriate initial letter or if he states a word that has already been used.

3. Players must make good passes of the potato word card to other players.

4. The winner is the last player left in the circle.

   Variations of the game: Play with the letters of the potato word card in sequence so that the first player uses the initial letter, the second player must think of a word that begins with the second letter, the next uses the third letter, and so forth.

Telephone Picture Tag: A variation of the game telephone, in which a message is passed from one player to another. At the end, the various changes in the message are shared. This is noncompetitive language play.

Purpose: To represent a message by a drawing and then to attempt to figure out the message based on the drawing.

Materials: Sufficient number of pencils for all players, a stack of three-inch paper squares for each player. The number of paper squares in each stack must correspond to the number of players in the game.

Preparation: Cut blank paper into three-inch squares. Ascertain the number of players there will be in a round of play. If there are nine players, then each player must have a stack of nine squares (a total of eighty-one squares would be needed to play the game). Supply pencils for each player.

Directions:

1. Players sit around a table. Although there is technically no limit to the number of players, the game works best with six to ten participants.

2. Once all players have paper and pencil, the group takes a few moments to think of a short famous quotation or title of a book, movie, or song.

3. Write the quote or title on the top square of paper.

4. At the command, "Ready, Pass!", each player passes the entire stack of papers with the quote or title to the person on their right.

5. After receiving a new stack, players should read the quote or title silently to themselves. (It is essential to read silently so as not to tip off other players about the quote or title.)

6. Place the quote or title on the bottom of the stack.

7. Draw a picture that represents what the quote or title means.

8. At the command, "Ready, Pass!", each player passes the entire stack of papers to the person on their right. This time, the paper square on top is the picture.

9. Look only at the picture and try to figure out what it represents. Do not look at the other papers for clues.

10. Place the picture on the bottom of the stack.

11. Each player writes the words that tell, to the best of their ability, what the picture represented.

12. Each time the stack is passed, the play alternates between writing words and drawing pictures.

13. Continue to play until each stack of paper squares returns to the original player.

14. Finish the game by having each player share the original message and the various drawings and permutations of the original quote or title. The fun is in seeing the crazy way the message was changed.

Rules:

1. Keep all stacks of paper together and moving in the same direction.

2. Avoid taking too much time to write or draw.

3. No peeking at the words or pictures within a stack until the end of the game.

Variations of the game: Specify at the outset of the game a category for a round of play, such as "song titles." Another approach would be to limit the category to a specific area of study, such as "U.S. History: Civil War Period."

In the movie *Dead Poets Society*, John Keating, the English teacher played by Robin Williams, asks the students, "What is the purpose of learning language and poetry?" After the students make several nominal attempts to respond to his question, he provides a comical answer, ". . . to woo women." A decidedly chauvinistic comment; but the point to note here is that language by its very nature is social-interactive. Using wordplay and humor emphasizes the social-interactive aspect of language usage. Social interaction is a key pedagogical component to language development. Helping ELLs develop language requires creating situations in which they can interact with one another according to their level of proficiency.

Matching Questions and Responses to Levels of Proficiency

As instructional strategies, questioning and responding date back to antiquity; however, for ELLs to develop listening and speaking skills teachers need to form appropriate questions and frame responses to match levels of proficiency. Questions have been ordered in a hierarchy according to cognitive levels. One of the most common ways to order questions is according to Bloom's (1968) taxonomy of higher-order thinking. Ideally, as teachers, we seek to move students from responding to simple factual information to synthesis. The challenge that arises is that in order to respond appropriately to higher-order questions, conventional wisdom dictates that the ELL needs to be more fluent in English. The problem that this creates is the false impression that until ELLs are fluent, they cannot participate in higher-order thinking. If the ELL is only able to speak in one- to two-word phrases, an open-ended question is not appropriate. Consequently, the ELL is not asked to consider higher-order questions. The truth is, however, that there are ways to structure questions and responses that encourage higher-order thinking.

Think about Bloom's taxonomy for a moment. Synthesis, the highest level of question according to Bloom, actually requires very few words. In the same way that a newspaper headline can synthesize a lengthy article, a student can synthesize a concept, a story, or an article. Synthesis can be demonstrated by a phrase with as few as one to three words. What this means is that higher-order thinking can take place even though the ELL is at a lower level of fluency. What the teacher must provide is an accessible way for the student to respond.

Here are three ways to help ELLs respond to a synthesis question: highlighting key words; creating a synthesis word bank; and inviting students to talk among themselves in their primary language.

Highlighting Key Words

A simple way to facilitate synthesis is to ask ELLs to highlight key words in a story or article. Key words would be the words that appear to be the most meaningful. Key words can be highlighted by using a marking pen or colored pencil, or by simply copying them on a separate piece of paper. Collect the highlighted words and write them on a chart. Then ask the students to pick three words that embody the message of the story or article.

Generating a Synthesis Word Bank

Another way to facilitate synthesis is to generate a word bank. Prior to asking a synthesizing question, solicit descriptive phrases from the entire class. Write the various random phrases on the board or on chart paper, to make a word bank. Then ask the synthesizing question and let students use the word bank to formulate written responses of their syntheses. The basis for this strategy is that each classroom contains a range of students at various levels of English proficiency; a word bank strategy draws on the knowledge and fluency of the entire group. Students at lower levels of proficiency can utilize the words that were generated by more proficient English speakers.

Inviting Primary Language Discussion

This strategy is simple in that it requires no special preparation. It is just a matter of inviting students at selected points in a lesson to talk to their same-language neighbor to paraphrase the learning thus far. Then follow by asking those who are able to translate their thinking into English for the whole group.

> ***Tip for parent involvement:*** Encourage students to interview family members regularly about subjects being taught at school. Provide basic interview questions that match the topic. Have the students take notes like a reporter and report back to class the following day.

Just because a student is unable to discuss a concept in depth in English does not mean that she is unable to conceptualize it in her primary language. The fundamental notion here is that thinking is not bound by a specific language. Could you imagine someone claiming that you can only solve math problems in English? It sounds ludicrous. Conversely, have you ever noticed a bilingual person switching to a dominant language to work out a complex problem? The same thinking applies to this strategy. Rather than seeing language diversity as a "barrier," begin to see other languages as different paths to knowledge and understanding.

References

Asher, J. (1982). *Learning another language through actions: The complete teacher's guidebook.* Los Gatos, CA: Sky Oaks.

Bloom, B. (1968). Learning for mastery. *Evaluation Comment, 1*(2). Los Angeles, CA: University of California, Los Angeles Center for the Study of Evaluation and Instructional Programs.

Douglass, M. (1989). *The reading process.* New York: Teachers College Press.

4

Teaching the Mechanics of Handwriting, Grammar, and Spelling

TESOL Goals and Standards

    GOAL 2: *To use English to achieve academically in all content areas*

    Standard 1: *Students will use English to interact in the classroom*

    Standard 2: *Students will use English to obtain, process, contruct, and provide subject matter information in spoken and written form*

One might ask, when is it appropriate to teach handwriting, grammar, and spelling? A more precise question is the following: What strategies help English Language Learners learn handwriting, grammar, and spelling at beginning, intermediate, and advanced stages? Fundamentally, instructional strategies must take into account the proficiency level of the student as well utilize the student's words as a starting point before moving to more abstract approaches (see Table 4.1).

TABLE 4.1 *Language Mechanics across Levels of Proficiency*

Conventions	*Beginning and Early Intermediate*	*Intermediate*	*Early Advanced/Advanced*
Handwriting	• Modeling	• When to use upper- • Sort letters by shape • Total Physical Response	• Font selection and lowercase
Grammar	• Modeling grammar in context	• The world's shortest	• Prepositional phrases sentences • Color-coded word walls
Spelling	• Letter and word recognition	• Word sorts and word building	• Word study

Handwriting

Handwriting is composed of various elements. According to Barbe, Wasylyk, Hackney, and Braun (1984), the elements are letter formation, size and proportion, spacing, slant, alignment, and line quality. There is also a sequence to letter formation. Generally letters are formed from top to bottom and left to right. Although teaching handwriting takes place in the primary grades, some newly arrived immigrant students at any grade level may not be familiar with Western script. They may need to be taught handwriting as part of letter recognition and formation.

Sort Letters By Shape

Rather than teach handwriting in alphabetical order, sort the letters by shape for lower- and uppercase. When the letters are sorted by shape, they become grouped according to similar strokes. This facilitates teaching letter formation. Note that there are basically lines, circles, curves, angles, and various combinations thereof. Also note the differences when sorting by lower- and uppercase. Some letters change their shape combinations.

Begin by teaching the straight-lined letters. It is an easy adjustment for students to follow with angled letters. Then teach circle-based letters, and then curves.

Letters Sorted by Shape and Case

Fundamental Letter Shape	*Lowercase*	*Uppercase*
Line	l t i	L T I E F H
Angle	v w x y k z	A M N V W X Y K Z
Circle/Line	o a b d p q	O Q
Open circle	c e	C G
Line/Half-circle		B D P R
Curved	h m n u	U
Partial curve	f r j g	J
S-curve	s	S

Use of Total Physical Response

Total Physical Response (TPR) is very useful for teaching letter shapes. TPR relies on physical actions in the form of demonstrated commands to orient oneself to letter formation.

Imagine the dotted line in the middle of a writing line (see illustration) as your belt, or waistline, with the top line across your forehead, and the bottom line at your feet. Using the body to orient the writing space on the paper, the teacher can give TPR commands to actively demonstrate letter formation. Give TPR commands that draw an imaginary line from head to toe. For example, for a lower-case "l," say, "Touch your head. Reach for your toes."

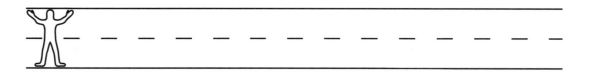

Begin each handwriting lesson with a TPR activity to actively demonstrate letter formation. Keep in mind that block print letters are generally formed from top to bottom and left to right. Write the TPR commands on charts to display on the walls with the proper formation of each letter. The following commands are grouped according to the fundamental shapes of the lower- and uppercase letters as illustrated above.

Tip for parent involvement: Show parents the following TPR commands to practice at home with their children. Make letter cards with the TPR commands on the opposite side. Use the cards like a game. Show a letter card and ask the child to demonstrate the actions.

Total Physical Response Commands for Straight-Lined Letters

Lowercase

l: Touch your head.
　Reach for your shoes.

t: Touch your head.
　Cross at the shoulders.

i: Touch your belt.
　Reach for your shoes.
　Dot it above the belt.

Uppercase

L: Touch your left ear.
　Reach for your left shoe.
　Cross to the right at your toes.

T: Touch your head.
　Reach, down the middle, for your toes.
　Cross at your head.

I: Touch your head.
　Reach for your toes.

E: Touch your left ear.
　Reach for your left shoe.
　Touch your left ear.
　Cross to the right.
　Touch your left side.
　Cross to the right.
　Touch your left shoe.
　Cross to the right.

F: Touch your left ear.
　Reach for your left shoe.
　Touch your left ear.
　Cross to the right.
　Touch your left side.
　Cross to the right.

H: Stand with feet apart.
　Touch your left ear.
　Reach for your left shoe.
　Touch your right ear.
　Reach for your right shoe.
　Cross it at the belt.

Total Physical Response Commands for Angled Letters

Lowercase

k: Stand with feet apart.
　Touch your left ear.
　Reach for your left shoe.
　Touch your right shoulder.
　Reach for your left side.
　Reach for your right shoe.

w: Touch your left side.
　Reach for your left foot.
　Touch your belt.
　Reach for your right shoe.
　Touch your right side.
　Reach for your right shoe.

v: Stand with feet together.
　Touch your left side.
　Reach between your shoes.
　Touch your right side.
　Reach for the ground.

x: Stand with feet apart.
 Touch your left side.
 Cross over to reach for
 your right foot.
 Touch your right side.
 Cross over to reach for
 left foot.

z: Stand with feet apart.
 Touch your left side.
 Cross it at the belt.
 Cross over to reach for your left shoe.
 Cross it to the right at your shoes.

y: Stand with feet together.
 Touch your left side.
 Reach for your shoes.
 Touch your right side.
 Reach below your shoes.

Uppercase

A: Stand with feet apart.
 Touch the top of your head.
 Reach for your left shoe.
 Touch the top of your head.
 Reach for your right shoe.
 Cross it at the belt.

N: Stand with feet apart.
 Touch your left ear. Reach for
 your left foot.
 Touch your left ear again.
 Cross over to your right foot.
 Touch your right ear.
 Reach for your right foot.

X: Stand with feet apart.
 Touch your left ear.
 Cross over to reach your
 right shoe.
 Touch your right ear.
 Cross over to reach
 your left shoe.

K: Stand with feet apart.
 Touch your left ear.
 Reach to your left shoe.
 Touch your right ear.
 Reach to your left side.
 Reach from your left side
 to your right shoe.

V: Stand with feet together.
 Touch your left ear.
 Reach for the middle, between
 your shoes.
 Touch your right ear.
 Reach for the middle, between
 your shoes.

Y: Stand with feet together.
 Touch your left ear.
 Cross over to the middle
 of your belt.
 Touch your right ear.
 Cross over to the middle
 of your belt.
 Reach from your belt to
 your shoes.

M: Stand with feet apart.
 Touch your left ear.
 Reach for your left shoe.
 Touch your left ear.
 Reach for the middle,
 between your shoes.
 Touch your right ear.
 Reach for the middle,
 between your shoes.
 Touch your right ear.
 Reach for your right shoe.

W: Stand with feet slightly apart.
 Touch your left ear.
 Reach for your left shoe.
 Touch the top of your head.
 Reach for your left shoe again.
 Touch the top of your head.
 Reach for your right shoe.
 Touch your right ear.
 Reach for your right shoe.

Z: Stand with feet apart.
 Touch your left ear.
 Cross to the right ear.
 Cross over to your left
 shoe.
 Cross to your right shoe.

Total Physical Response Commands for Circle/Line Letters

Lowercase

o: Touch your belt in the
 middle.
 Reach down to make a circle
 to the left.
 Touch your shoes before
 curving up to the belt.

a: Touch your belt in the middle.
 Reach down to make a circle to the left.
 Touch your shoes before curving up to
 the belt.
 Touch your right side.
 Reach to your right shoe.

b: Touch your left ear.
 Reach for your left shoe.
 Touch your belt in the
 middle.
 Reach down to make a
 circle to the left.
 Touch your shoes before
 curving up to the belt.

d: Touch your belt in the middle.
  Reach down to make a circle
  to the left.
  Touch your shoes before
  curving up to the belt.
  Touch your right ear.
  Reach for your right shoe.

p: Touch your left side.
  Reach down below your left shoe.
  Touch your belt in the middle.
  Reach down to make a circle to the left.
  Touch your shoes before curving up
  to the belt.

q: Touch your belt in the
  middle.
  Reach down to make a
  circle to the left.
  Touch your shoes before
  curving up to the belt.
  Touch your right side.
  Reach down below your
  right shoe.

Uppercase

O: Touch the top of your head.
  Curve a circle to the left.
  Touch your shoes before curving
  up to your head.

Q: Touch the top of your head.
  Curve a circle to the left.
  Touch your shoes before curving up to your head.
  Touch your belt in the middle.
  Squiggle a line to your right shoe.

Total Physical Response Commands for Open Circle Letters

Lowercase

c: Touch your right leg just above
  the knee.
  Curve around to the left.
  Touch your shoes.
  Stop the curve just before your
  right knee.

e: Touch your right leg just above the knee.
  Curve to the left around at the belt.
  Curve down and touch your shoes.
  Stop the curve just before your right knee.
  Cross to the left.
  Stop at your left leg.

Uppercase

C: Touch your right shoulder.
  Curve up to the left.
  Touch the top of your head.
  Touch your left side.
  Touch your shoes.
  Stop at your right knee.

G: Touch your right shoulder.
  Curve up to the left.
  Touch the top of your head.
  Touch your left side.
  Touch your shoes.
  Stop at your right side.
  Cross to the left at the belt.

Total Physical Response Commands for Curved Letters

Lowercase

h: Stand with feet apart.
  Touch your left ear.
  Reach to your left shoe.
  Touch your left side just below the belt.
  Curve up to the right.
  Touch the belt.
  Curve down to your right shoe.

m: Stand with feet apart.
  Touch your left side at the belt.
  Reach down to your left shoe.
  Curve up and touch your belt.
  Curve to the middle between your shoes.
  Curve up to your belt.
  Curve down to your right shoe.

n: Stand with feet apart.
   Touch your left side at the belt.
   Reach down to your left shoe.
   Curve up and touch your belt.
   Reach down to your right shoe.

u: Stand with feet apart.
   Touch your left side at the belt.
   Reach down to your left shoe.
   Curve over to your right shoe.
   Reach up to your right side at the belt.
   Reach back down to your right shoe.

Uppercase

U: Touch your left ear.
   Reach down to your left shoe.
   Curve over to your right shoe.
   Reach up to your right ear.

Total Physical Response Commands for Letters Formed from Lines and Half-Circles

Uppercase (only)

B: Touch your left ear.
   Reach down to your left shoe.
   Touch your left ear again.
   Curve down to the right.
   Cross at the belt.
   Curve down to the right from the belt.
   Cross your shoes.
   Stop at your left shoe.

D: Touch your left ear.
   Reach down to your left shoe.
   Touch your left ear again.
   Make a big curve to the right.
   Cross your shoes.
   Stop at your left shoe.

P: Touch your left ear.
   Reach down to your left shoe.
   Touch your left ear again.
   Curve down to the right.
   Cross at the belt.

R: Touch your left ear.
   Reach down to your left shoe.
   Touch your left ear again.
   Curve down to the right.
   Cross at the belt.
   Cross over from the belt to your right shoe.

Total Physical Response Commands for Partially Curved Letters

Lowercase

f: Start at the middle, above the belt.
   Curve down to the left shoe.
   Cross at the belt.

r: Touch your left side.
   Reach down to your left shoe.
   Touch the belt at the middle.
   Curve down to the left side.

j: Start at the middle of your belt.
   Reach down below your shoes and
   curve to the left.
   Dot it in the middle above the belt.

g: Touch your belt in the middle.
   Reach down to make a circle to the left.
   Touch your shoes before curving up to the belt.
   Touch your right side.
   Reach below your shoes.
   Curve to the left below your shoes.

Uppercase

J: Touch your right ear.
   Reach down to your shoes.
   Curve up to the left.
   Stop at your knee.

Total Physical Response Commands for the S-Curve Letters

Lowercase

s: Start on your right side, just below the belt.
   Curve up across the belt.
   Curve down across the knees.
   Touch your right shoe.
   Curve up across your shoes.
   Stop at the knees.

Uppercase

S: Touch your right ear.
   Curve over your head to the left.
   Touch your left shoulder.
   Curve down to the right across your belt.
   Curve down to your right knee.
   Curve to the left across your shoes.
   Stop at your left knee.

Grammar

There is a strong connection between oral and written language; however, the two are not entirely synonymous. According to King and Rentel (1981), children in grades one through four tended to write in much the same way that they spoke. With ELLs the use of primary language syntax in English is prevalent. Sulzby and Teale (2003) argued that instruction of conventional grammar in written language is required to help children sort out the differences between oral and written language.

The World's Shortest Sentence

Using hyperbole with regard to writing can illustrate a fundamental aspect about grammar, that a sentence is composed of a noun phrase + verb phrase.
   Directions:

1. Divide the class into small groups of four students each.
2. Ask each group to compose and write down the shortest sentence that they can possibly think of.
3. Allow two to three minutes for the group work.
4. As groups compose their sentences, have them write them on the board. (This gives the whole class a small number of sentences to analyze, yet each member of the class has provided input.)

5. Ask every student to write down the sentences as they appear on the board.
6. Begin to analyze the sentences:
   - Which one is the shortest?
   - Is it a complete sentence? Explain your understanding of a complete sentence.
   - What words can be taken out to make it shorter, yet still complete?
7. Once you analyze and shorten a sentence as a whole group, ask the students to shorten the other sentences. Challenge them to get the sentences down to two words.
8. Ultimately, students will pare them down to sentences as short as "She ran." At this point, ask students the following: What are the components of a complete sentence? (Be prepared for the students that form a command such as "Go!" Ask them if it is a complete sentence and to explain their thinking as to why it is complete or not.)
9. As students will soon discover, a sentence is composed of a noun phrase plus a verb phrase. This simple discovery raises their level of awareness about the make-up of a sentence fragment or a complete sentence.
10. Now ask them to identify the noun phrase and verb phrase in other sentences.

Color Code Parts of Speech

When developing a word wall for a classroom, consider color coding parts of speech. Use different colored word cards for each part of speech. For example, display nouns on yellow cards, verbs on blue, adjectives on red, and adverbs on green. Make a legend for the color coding to be displayed next to the word wall.

Tip for parent involvement: Make up color-coded noun phrase cards and verb phrase cards. Ask parents to play a game with the cards by combining noun and verb phrases to make complete sentences. Also color code parts of speech cards to combine words into complete sentences.

Teach Prepositions as Phrases

Think about the baffling nature of prepositions. We ride *in* a car, but *on* an airplane. Teaching prepositions in isolation does not account for their situational usage; teaching prepositions in a phrase does not necessarily explain why we use them in a particular way, but it provides some contextual usage.

Spelling

Spelling in English poses many problems. Conventional spelling is determined by social and historical factors rather than by a prescribed system of logical rules. Nevertheless, there are certain ways to understand the acquisition of spelling proficiency as a developmental process. Gentry (1987) posited an organization of spelling in developmental stages. This organization provides a way to understand how students will spell a word like "monster" as representational scribble and pictures, as a collection of consonants like *mtr*, as an idiosyncratic invention like *munstr* or *mostar*, or finally as a conventionally accepted norm *monster.*

The developmental stages for spelling according to Gentry (1987) are precommunicative, semiphonetic, phonetic, transitional, conventional, and morphemic/syntactic. Briefly, the precommunicative stage is characterized by representational scribble and drawings of caricatures.

Semiphonetic spellings include letters that indicate dominant sounds in words. Phonetic spellings use a vowel in each syllable, but are idiosyncratic, inventive spellings. Transitional spellings are characterized by misspellings that do not have a phonetic quality. Conventional spellings are those agreed upon by our culture as normative. Finally, morphemic/syntactic spellers master the language to the point where they can manipulate words accurately for their own intentions.

Table 4.2 shows the various stages of developmental spelling and how the stages map on to corresponding levels of English Language Development (ELD) with appropriate strategies for each level.

TABLE 4.2 *The Stages of Developmental Spelling and Levels of English Language Development*

Developmental Stage	Descriptors	Examples	Corresponding ELD Level (Recommended Strategies)
Precommunicative	• Scribbling can be representational • Understands speech can be written • Lacks concept of a word • Makes letterlike shapes • May write name	(random scribbles, marks, or drawings)	**Beginning** (Strategies: letter and word recognition)
Semiphonetic (*Rule of thumb:* Not a plausible word structure in English: e.g. CCC)	• Spells few words correctly but knows letters make words • Still invents symbols for letters and words • Makes 1- to 3-letter representations of words, usually consonants • Has more control over beginnings and endings of words • Predicts words auditorially in frequently occurring patterns	*mtr*	**Beginning, Early Intermediate** (Strategies: letter and word recognition, word sorting)
Phonetic (*Rule of thumb:* Plausible structure for a word in English: e.g. CVCV)	• Spellings include all sound features of words as heard. • Invents system of phonetic spelling that is consistent • Understands relationship of sounds in speech to symbols in writing • Spelling can be read by others	*mostar* *monstr*	**Early Intermediate, Intermediate** (Strategies: word sorts, identify structural patterns, word families)
Transitional (*Rule of thumb:* May appear as a typo; no auditory distinction)	• Begins to spell conventionally and knows it is necessary for others to read their writing • Uses knowledge of how words look as well as sound and applies this to other words • Includes vowels in every syllable	*monstar* *monstur* *monstir* *monstor*	**Early Advanced** (Strategies: continue word sorts, patterns, families; add word study, systematic rule building)

Developmental Stage	Descriptors	Examples	Corresponding ELD Level (Recommended Strategies)
	• Uses familiar spelling patterns. • Intersperses conventional spelling with invented spelling		
Conventional	• Begins to spell correctly • Has mastered root words, past tense, and short vowels • Still struggles with consonant doubling, letter position, and word affixes • Has growing knowledge of word meanings and complicated vowel patterns	*monster*	**Early Advanced, Advanced** (Strategies: word study, systematic rule building, etymologies, roots, parts of speech)
Morphemic/ Syntactic	• Increasingly understands how meaning and grammatical structure control spelling • Adds morphemic and syntactic knowledge to phonological knowledge • Is better at doubling consonants, spelling alternative forms of words, and word endings • Conducts wordplay in creative ways	"Monster, schmonster, it doesn't scare me."	**Advanced** (Strategies: same as above; encourage wordplay)

Rules of Thumb

At first, it may appear difficult to differentiate semiphonetic, phonetic, and transitional spellings. Use the following guidelines to help identify unique features of the spellings. For semiphonetic spellings, the rule of thumb is that it is not a plausible structure of a word in English. For example, many semiphonetic spellings are a collection of consonants with no vowels, as in *mtr* for monster. No plausible word in English will have three consonants without vowels in between; in English each syllable needs a vowel.

For phonetic spelling, conversely, the rule of thumb is that the spelling has a plausible structure of a word in English, such as CVCV. The phonetic spellings are not conventional, but they are decodable. Phonetic spellers will spell multisyllabic words in creative ways; for example, the word *attention* might be spelled *atenshun*. There is a certain logic to phonetic spelling. The spelling follows a conventional structure, but the spelling is invented. Each syllable will have a vowel sound, although final consonants that have a vowel quality such as *r* or *l* may not carry a vowel. Examples of this are *monstr* for monster or *lidl* for little.

For transitional spelling, the rule of thumb is that it looks like a typo (a single letter misplaced) and that the variance is not phonetic or auditory. Generally speaking, transitional spellers use conventional spelling for most words; however, double consonants, silent *e*, *wh*-, and homophones are particularly problematic. Examples of transitional spellings are as follows: double consonants, *little/litle*; silent *e, time/tim* or *with/withe*; words using *wh, which/wich*; homophones, *right/write*. In each example the variance is not attributed to an auditory feature of the word. One does not hear a consonant doubled in medial position, a silent *e*, the *h* in *which*, or the difference between *right* and *write*. These are characteristics that need to be recognized by sight.

Activities to Address Spelling

The following spelling activities are arranged to correspond to stages of developmental spelling and ELD levels of fluency. Note that there is some overlap between the two systems.

Letter/word recognition. (Spelling stages: precommunicative/semiphonetic; ELD levels: beginning/early intermediate)

Match picture cards with letters in initial position. Develop a picture card file. Order the file according to the alphabet. On one side of the cards glue pictures cut from magazines. You can even have the students help by selecting pictures to cut out and glue. On the other side, write the initial letter that represents the picture with the word. File the pictures in a box with dividers for each letter of the alphabet.

Make an accompanying set of letter cards and word cards that match the pictures in the file. Students can either look for pictures that match a specific letter or find the right letter to match the picture.

Use a sand tray to give students the opportunity to practice writing upper- and lowercase letters that match the pictures in the file. A sand tray is simply a rectangular tray like a cookie sheet. Pour an even layer of fine grain sand (salt can be substituted) in the tray. Allow students to finger-spell letters and words. Follow the finger-spelling with a practice writing activity on lined paper.

Word sorts. (Spelling stages: phonetic/early transitional; ELD levels: early intermediate/ intermediate)

Use a word wall to list words according to the same initial letter. Make the word wall with a large wall space and yarn. Use the yarn to lay out a grid for each letter of the alphabet. Configure the grid as a five-row, five-column square, and then add one more space for *z*.

Each time the group learns a new word, ask a student to make a word for the word wall. Allow the student the opportunity to figure out the appropriate space on the word wall for the card. Consider making a poster-sized word wall grid. Give the students a stack of high-frequency words and ask them to place them in the appropriate spaces on the grid.

Alpha strips for alphabetizing words. To help beginning or early intermediate students, have them make their own alpha strips. Give each student a tag board strip, twenty-six inches long, with inch marks. Direct the students to fill in the letters in the right order, one per inch.

Give students a stack of word cards to place in alphabetical order. Begin with initial letters and then make the alpha sorting more complex with words that have the same initial letter so that the students will have to refer to the second, third, or fourth letter.

Word search for common structures. Make up a series of cards that represent common word structures using arrangements of consonants and vowels, for example, CVC, CVCV, CCVC, and so forth. Create a table with multiple columns. Label each column with a different common structure. Give the students a selected text to conduct a word search.

Hold up one of the cards, such as CVC, and ask the students to read through the selected text to find as many words as possible that have that structure (e.g., cat, bat, log, jog). To add motivation and fun, establish teams and a time limit. See which team can find the most words according to the stated structures. Record the findings on the table under the appropriate subheading.

A variation of this activity is to ask students to make up what they think are plausible structures of words in English using the C-V coding. Ask teams to challenge one another to find the "hidden" word(s) in the text that use that structure.

Tip for parent involvement: Give parents a list of English word structures using the C-V coding. Ask them to search through a newspaper and clip out the words that match each structure.

Word families with r-controlled vowels (-ar, -er, -ir, -or, -ur). Create cluster maps to identify words that belong in the same r-controlled vowel group.

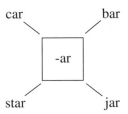

Word building. (Spelling stages: phonetic/early transitional; ELD levels: early intermediate/ intermediate)

Word-building activities put together whole or parts of words to form new words. There are limitless possibilities, but the following activities are some that will be used frequently.

Onsets and rimes. Forming onsets and rimes is another way to explore word families. A very common word family is made from the rime *-ake*. A wide variety of onsets can be placed in front of *-ake* to form words with similar structure such as *bake, cake, fake, Jake.*

A way to give students the opportunity to explore onsets and rimes is to make a vertical strip with the alphabet written sequentially from top to bottom. Then make a series of cards with rimes. For the rime cards, you can simply leave a space for the onset (vertical alphabet strip) or you can cut a window in the card for the onset to pass through. Either way, students will line up the vertical alphabet strip against a rime card and begin to form words. Some of the words will be nonsense words; for example, the onset *z-* and the rime *-ake* makes the nonsense word *zake*. To deal with nonsense words as opposed to actual words, make a T-graph as a comparative table to record them.

Add to the activity by making vertical strips with consonant blend onsets such as *ch-, sh-, bl-,* and *gr-*. Ask students to create their own vertical onset strips and rime cards. Again, compare plausible structures with ones that never occur in English.

Prefix, root, and suffix guided construction. This activity addresses the relationship of prefixes, roots, and suffixes. It requires a three-column table and three sets of word cards. First make a three-column table with the headings of prefix, root, and suffix.

Prefix	Root	Suffix

Make a series of prefix cards. On one side write the prefix, such as *pre-*. On the opposite side of the card write the definition of the prefix, such as *"pre- means before."* You can get a comprehensive listing of prefixes from any quality dictionary.

Make a series of root word cards. Write cards in lowercase letters because you will be affixing word parts to the front of the roots. On one side, write the root word. On the opposite side, write the definition and include a sketch when appropriate.

The difficult task with this activity is to make the suffix cards. The reason is that affixing suffixes sometimes requires a change in the spelling of the root word. (See the spelling rules below for some of the changes.) In making the suffix cards, you will need to include all the variations of a particular suffix, for example *-ion, -tion, -sion,* and so forth. Like the prefixes, look up suffix in a quality dictionary to get a comprehensive list.

Once the table and card sets are made, students can use the materials to build words. At first, it is highly recommended that this be a guided activity because so many of the suffix conversions are not intuitive. Another reason for guiding the exploration with this activity is that the meanings of the words will change considerably with affixes. Initially the teacher may need to clarify the meaning of words and also explain which are actual words in the lexicon and which are created by the exploratory activity.

Word study. (Spelling stages: transitional/conventional/morphemic-syntactic; ELD levels: early advanced/advanced)

Teaching explicit spelling rules. Viswamohan (2004) identified ten spelling rules that are particularly baffling to English learners. It is probably safe to say that they are baffling to native English speakers as well. These rules need to be taught explicitly because they are not intuitive and defy logical patterns. The ten rules are as follows:

1. What comes first, *i* or *e*? The common rule "i before e, except after c" has almost as many exceptions as words that follow the rule. For example achieve, deceive, heinous, protein, fief, receive. There are two ways to approach this rule. One is to simply teach the *ei* words as a word family. The other way is to conduct word searches in context for examples of *ei* or *ie* words.

2. Replace *y* with *i* or *e* when a word ends in a consonant plus *y*. Two aspects govern this rule: the part of speech and the specific inflected ending of the word. Inflected endings are *-s, -ly, -er, -est, -ed*. Create a table to show the relationships among parts of speech, inflections, and rules.

Part of Speech and Inflection	Retain -y-	Change to -i-	Change to -ie-	Change -ie- to -y-
Nouns **-s**	Plurals after a vowel: survey > surveys		Plurals after a consonant: baby > babies	
Adjectives **-er** **-est**		Comparatives: early > earlier, earliest		
Adverbs **-ly**		Adverbs formed from adjectives: busy > busily		
Verbs **-ed** **-ing**	Before -ing: copy > copying	Past-tense ending with a consonant +y: cry > cried		Before -ing: die > dying

3. Silent *-e* in final position indicates a "long" vowel sound. Examples are *made, theme, time, lode,* and *cute.* There are numerous exceptions to this rule, however. Some exceptions are words ending in *-nse* or *-nce* such as *tense* or *mince.* One of the best ways to teach this rule is to have students conduct a word search in a selected text to find as many examples of silent *-e* as possible. Use a T-table to note words that follow the rule and those that are exceptions.

4. The reasons for consonant doubling. Essentially consonant doubling is to indicate the vowel sound as follows: a long vowel with a single consonant, as in "hoping," and a short vowel sound with consonant doubling, as in "hopping." It also indicates stress on a syllable such as with "recur" and "recurrence." Also, the letters *y*, *w*, and *x* are not doubled.

Consonant doubling is confusing because of the way we describe vowels as long or short. "Long and short vowels" do not refer to the length of a sound. They are arbitrary descriptors at best and are inaccurate ways to describe vowel sounds. More accurately, the stress on a syllable describes the length of the sound. Say the word "forbidden" aloud. Note that the stress is on the second syllable "for-*bid*-den." You can accentuate the stress by saying the word slowly, "f o r-*B I D*-d e n." When you say it slowly, note how the stressed syllable is actually longer in duration than the other syllables. Making this distinction will help students understand the function of the double consonant to indicate stress.

To help students visualize the stress on a syllable, use a gesture. Touch your hands together at the fingertips. Speak a word aloud and slowly. As you say a stressed syllable in the word, pull your hands apart to indicate the length of the stress. Try it with the following words: *M A R*-ket (market), for-*G E T*-ting, pre-*F E R R E D.*

5. The emergence of the schwa in medial position. A feature unique to English that poses problems for transitional spellers is the placement of appropriate vowels in the middle of a multi-syllabic words. In English speech with multisyllabic words, medial vowels convert, by default, to a schwa sound. The schwa sound has been described as *uh,* like a cartoon caveman saying, "*ugh.*" This *uh* sound is evident in two syllable words like "*bu*tter," three syllable words such as "re*a*lize," and in words with more syllables such as "char*ac*terize." No matter the spelling, the schwa sound emerges in the middle of words. The specific letters used for conventional spelling

do not necessarily correspond to the letter sound. Therefore, transitional spellers will often misplace a vowel in multisyllabic words.

An activity that Viswamohan (2004) suggested is to use clue words to help identify the appropriate spelling of potentially problematic words.

Problem Word	Clue Word	Hidden Vowel
defin_te	definition	i
rep_tition	repeat	e
exam_nation	examine	i

6. Using the right suffix, *-able* or *-ible*. As a general rule, a word like "adaptable" can stand on its own if the suffix *-able* is removed; while the word "feasible" is not a free standing word once the suffix *-ible* is removed. To teach the rule, therefore, is to ask the students to play with the morphology of the words and to break them into parts to test if they require *-able* or *-ible*.

7. Using *-ous* or *-us*. The schwa factor comes into play here. The two structures sound alike because they default to a schwa sound. The key is to teach parts of speech in conjunction with these word endings. Create a T-table showing adjectives and nouns. Also, the adjectives are complete words without the suffix *-ous*, whereas *-us* on the nouns is part of the word.

Adjectives	Nouns
amorous	fungus
dangerous	status
hazardous	nexus

8. Using *-er* or *-or*. The r-controlled schwa poses problems for all spellers. As an aside, it seems like the Russians solved this problem by eliminating the vowel in words like "Petr." Alas, in English we have to use more complex means to spell verbs and nouns. But the rule only works most of the time.

-or Rule

Verbs	Nouns
create	creator
terminate	terminator
indicate	indicator
survey	surveyor
collect	collector
govern	governor

-er Exceptions

Verbs	Nouns
design	designer
mine	miner
sing	singer

9. Use of *-ion* at the end of a word in its various forms. This complex structure cannot be written as a rule. It is best to display a chart as a reminder to students. Remember that the purpose of the *-ion* suffix is to change a verb to a noun.

Types of word structures	*Variation of -ion*	*Examples of verb > noun change with -ion*
Verbs ending in *-t* or *–ct*	*-ion*	edit > edition, direct > direction
Verbs with the suffix *–ate*	*-tion*	migrate > migration
Verbs ending in *-mit, -ede, -eed, -ss, -rt, -end*	*-ssion* or *-sion*	transmit > transmission, concede > consession, succeed, succession, obsess > obsession, convert > conversion, comprehend > comprehension
Verbs ending in *-firm* or *-form*	*-ation*	confirm > confirmation, inform > information
Verbs with suffix *-fy* or *-ly*	*-ication*	glorify > glorification, imply > implication
Verbs with an *-ei-* pattern	*-eption*	receive > reception
Verbs ending in *-uce*	*-uction*	reduce > reduction
Verbs ending in *-ume*	*-umption*	consume > consumption
Verbs with suffix *-scribe*	*-ription*	inscribe > inscription

10. Silent consonants *h, p, g, n, k,* and *b,* at first glance, appear to have no function. To understand the use of silent consonants, it is vital to know the etymologies of the words that utilize these problematic structures. Many of our silent consonants are derived from Latin, Greek, and/or Norse roots. But sometimes the use of the silent consonant can only be explained as a phonological device that makes pronunciation less awkward.

The use of a silent *h* is the least problematic for Spanish speakers because of the same function in Spanish. Words with silent *h* like *honor* and *honest* correspond to cognates due to the Latin roots.

Greek roots utilize a silent *p* in words *like psychology, pneumonia,* and *pterodactyl.*

The use of silent *p* in the noun adjunct *cupboard,* however, simply reduces the awkwardness of trying to pronounce a *p* followed by a *b* in the same word. Notice the position of your lips as you speak . The *p* and *b* are the same position, which means you would have to pronounce the *p,* then open and close your mouth again to pronounce the *b.*

Other Greek-loaned silent letters are the *m* in the *mneumonic* and the *g* in *sign, gnat, gnome, phlegm,* and *foreign.* Curiously the *n* in final position is silent when proceeded by an *m* in words such as *solemn, autumn* and *condemn,* but when the words are used in a different form, the *n* is pronounced as in *condemnation.*

Norse influence in the language gives us a silent *k* when coupled with an *n* in initial position. Examples of this are *knot, knife, knuckle, knight, knead,* and *knee.* Approximately a half-dozen words in the entire English lexicon have this structure; therefore, it does not require a rule.

The silent *b* appears when it follows *m* in final position. Examples of silent *b* after *m* are *comb, numb, lamb,* and *tomb.* Note that the rule breaks down when *-er* is at the end. While *beachcomber* and *plumber* maintain a silent *b, amber* and *slumber* do not.

Create a personal thesaurus to explore multiple meanings (u/you/ewe). Creating a personal thesaurus gives the students the benefits of a personal dictionary, yet it is a living document. With a personal dictionary, once the definition is recorded a word is complete. With a personal thesaurus, the associations can grow as the student develops greater knowledge of the language.

To initiate a personal thesaurus, provide each student with a loose-leaf binder. Each page should begin as an empty cluster map. Have the student write a key word in the center of the cluster map. Around the center of the cluster-mapped key word, add words with related meanings.

Each week provide students with one or two key words for the center of the cluster maps. Also, give the students a blank cluster map page with the instructions that they are to find a key word to develop. Set aside a thesaurus development time each week and encourage students to read to find new words to add to the thesaurus. Encourage them also to compare notes with classmates to come up with other meanings to include. The cluster map format, being nonlinear, allows for numerous additions.

Tip for parent involvement: As part of a regular homework routine, ask parents to work with their child on developing their personal thesaurus. Begin the thesaurus at school, but once a week send it home. Use the same guidelines as above. Target words that are especially difficult for ELLs to spell.

Illustrate homophone pairs (sale/sail). Have students illustrate homophone pairs to differentiate them. Decorate the classroom with the illustrations, or bind them in a homophone pair picture book.

Illustrating homophone pairs is as simple as folding a piece of paper in half. Partner students by homophone pairs and give each one a word to illustrate.

Another approach to using illustrated homophone pairs is to play a mix and matching game. Once a student has illustrated a word, she must mingle with classmates to find the matching pair.

References

Barbe, W. B., Wasylyk, T. M., Hackney, C. S., & Braun, L. A. (1984). *Zaner-Bloser creative growth in handwriting* (grades K–8). Columbus, OH: Zaner-Bloser.

Gentry, J. R. (1987). *Spel . . . is a four-letter word.* Portsmouth, NH: Heinemann.

King, M., & Rentel, V. (1981). *How children learn to write: A longitudinal study.* (Final report to the National Institute of Education, RF Project 761861/71238 & 765512/711748). Columbus, OH: Ohio State University Research Foundation.

Sulzby, E., & Teale, W. H. (2003). The development of the young child and the emergence of literacy. In J. Flood, D. Lapp, J. R. Squire, & J. M. Jensen (Eds.). *Handbook of research on teaching the English Language Arts.* (2nd ed.) (pp. 300–313). Mahwah, NJ: Erlbaum.

Viswamohan, A. (May 2004). Putting students under the spell. *Language Magazine, 3*(9), pp. 14–17.

5

Vocabulary Development

TESOL Goals and Standards

GOAL 2: *To use English to achieve academically in all content areas*

Standard 1: *Students will use English to interact in the classroom*

Standard 2: *Students will use English to obtain, process, construct, and provide subject matter information in spoken and written form*

Have you ever noticed that we tend to teach vocabulary the way we were taught in school? Unfortunately, many of us were taught vocabulary in a very passive and abstract way. As students, we were asked to look up new terms in the glossary at the back of the text, or told to copy definitions from the dictionary and then memorize them. By the same token, I have yet to meet a person who enjoyed learning vocabulary by looking up glossary terms. As an initial approach to teaching English Language Learners, asking them to use glossaries or dictionary definitions is ineffective for vocabulary instruction. Teaching vocabulary to ELLs at early levels of fluency is even more challenging, and calls for a more strategic approach.

In this chapter, prior to looking at strategies, we must first understand vocabulary development from the perspective of the ELL. We will look at vocabulary as concrete, symbolic/representational, and abstract and explore ways to provide instruction at each level. Abstraction poses unique challenges to teaching ELLs; therefore, we will also look at ways to "unpack" the meaning in abstract words. Finally, we will examine ways to develop fluency with vocabulary once the meaning is established, with interactive games to develop fluency, digital flash cards using presentation software to practice high-frequency words, and developing descriptive continua.

Understanding Vocabulary Development from an English Language Learner's Perspective

In order to effectively teach vocabulary, it is helpful to understand how the unique perspective of the ELL calls for a range of strategies. First let's consider how literate, English-speaking adults perceive words in significantly different ways from ELLs. As literate adults, when we see a word such as *brilliant*, the word by itself appears to be quite meaningful. We see the combination of letters as meaningful because we involuntarily call to mind what the word represents. "Brilliant" conjures up images of light, intelligence, brightness, intense color, and so forth. In other words, literate, English-speaking adults automatically see words as inherently meaningful because they already know what the word means. Conversely, an ELL may look at the same combination of letters and see only letters without perceiving the images that give it meaning. The letter combinations by themselves are essentially abstract.

Meaning, therefore, is something apart from combining letters in a conventional sequence. Meaning is experiential, sensorial, and image driven. It is nonverbal. To illustrate, think of how a baby learns a word such as *hug*. A baby does not learn the word "hug" from a word card or glossary. A baby learns it through a concrete experience of hugging. In other words, the experience of meaning is initially nonverbal; the verbal label of "hug" is applied after the experience has taken place.

In much the same way, an ELL initially learns vocabulary through the senses. This is easily seen when we look at languages that use nonalphabetic systems. If you do not read Japanese, for instance, the characters appear to be abstract, random, and meaningless. Obviously, it would not be helpful to look at Japanese word cards in order to find meaning. To understand the meaning of the word in Japanese requires a demonstration or a meaningful experience first.

Curiously, some teachers begin vocabulary instruction in very abstract ways with word cards, glossaries, and so forth, thus assuming that looking at a word by itself is meaningful. However, teaching vocabulary from an abstraction without grounding it in a meaningful experience is ineffective teaching.

This is not to excoriate the use of word cards, but by themselves word cards cannot provide a meaningful experience. A more strategic use for word cards is to follow the experience as a label. Again, what comes first? The experience? Or its label? Remember the rule of thumb: "Show first; tell second."

A Range of Strategies for Making Vocabulary and Concepts Comprehensible

Learning from a concrete experience is not a new idea. It can be attributed to Dewey (1902) and Piaget (1926), and more recent work with vocabulary development strategies has been done by Chamot and O'Mally (1987). We learn by doing, by experiencing meaning. Based on an adaptation of Piagetian categories, items and techniques for teaching vocabulary instruction can be organized across a developmental continuum of three groupings: concrete, symbolic/ representational, and abstract.

Concrete	*Symbolic/Representational*	*Abstract*
Real objects (realia)	Pictures	Word cards
Meaningful Movement (TPR)	Symbols, icons	Sentence strips
Actual experiences	Visual aids	Oral explanations
Experiments	Maps	(w/o modeling)
Performance	Models	Theoretical discussion
Demonstration/modeling	Semantic maps	Decontextualized print
	Flowcharts	
	Illustrated books	

Concrete

Concrete techniques provide actual experiences of learning with the real object of study. These include providing real objects, or realia, that students can handle and explore with their senses. For example, a trip outside the classroom doors to a eucalyptus tree, to touch its shedding bark, smell its aromatic leaves, hear it creak in the wind, and see its height from different perspectives, teaches the word "eucalyptus" in a profound way. Nouns are taught with concrete objects, yet verbs are taught by meaningful actions. Total Physical Response (TPR), discussed in the previous chapter, gives students a concrete experience with verbs.

Although concrete instruction of vocabulary is extremely effective, the difficulty with concrete/experiential teaching is that sometimes it is impossible to provide the real object. For example, you are not going to bring a live cow into a classroom to teach the word "Holstein." Nor is it possible to go back in time to see real events in history as they unfolded. In those cases, it is helpful to utilize the symbolic level of teaching vocabulary.

Symbolic/Representational

Strategies on the symbolic level involve providing representations of the word to be taught: providing visuals to illustrate the meaning of a word, or a short digital video clip to supply more visual context. When real objects are not available or practical to utilize, provide a model. Some possible models include masks of historical or story characters, anatomical models (e.g. heart), layered models to show the atmosphere or the make-up of a planet, landscapes, cityscapes, or scenescapes.

Abstract

Abstraction is a strategy in language employed to conceptualize complex ideas, or to combine a variety of concepts into a key term for theory development. For example, when describing similar events in history, we label them as a trend. The function of the abstraction is that it allow one to discuss the multiple events using a single word. The prerequisite for abstraction is that all parties know what the term means. Therefore, it is incumbent upon the teacher to use concrete and symbolic strategies prior to moving into abstraction.

When and how to use word cards. Imagine a teacher holding up a word card without context clues and saying, "What do you think this means?" The fact that the question is raised, probably means that the students don't know what it means. So why ask the question?

Strategies for Vocabulary Development Across Levels of Proficiency

Choosing a Strategy

Although beginning English Language Learners will benefit from predominantly concrete instruction, this does not mean that they cannot understand abstract words. Conversely, advanced-level ELLs benefit significantly from concrete instruction. Choosing the appropriate strategy involves more than matching levels of proficiency. Judging the appropriateness of using concrete, symbolic, or abstract strategies requires knowing what to do with a particular word.

Some words lend themselves to the use of realia, while others do not. There are words in which a visual is the most appropriate strategy available. Additionally, there are words that are more conceptually abstract that can be "unpacked" in order to find their meaning at a concrete or representational level. Unpacking a conceptual word means exploring its multiple meanings and/or word origins to get to a more grounded understanding of its meaning. For example, in literary analysis, if one is teaching the term *denouement*, knowing its etymology is essential to illustrating the meaning. The word comes from the French term for untying a knot. The etymology provides a visual way to understand the term of how a plot is being disentangled.

Knowing a word, therefore, dictates the strategy. Here is a three-point test for a word in order to determine the appropriate strategy.

1. How can a real object or experience be used to teach the word?
2. How can a visual or model be used to teach the word?
3. Is the word conceptual or abstract? If so, select one or more unpacking strategies:
   - Check the etymology
   - Explore related roots
   - Discuss cognates
   - Provide primary language support
   - Use similes and metaphorical thinking with word study charts

Consider the range of strategies from concrete to abstract as building a foundation for meaning. To the extent possible, begin with concrete objects and experiences, follow with visuals or models, and then address the abstraction. The broader and deeper the concrete experience, the greater the degree of abstraction that can be attained in the long run. For example, a highly fluent ELL may have knowledge gaps in a specific subject area such as marine science; therefore, it would be appropriate to use realia and visuals as materials for instruction such as supplying pieces of coral or shells, or showing visuals such as a video to develop meaning. The concrete and visual instruction enhances instruction for all parties. Now that some background has been established, we will look at how the strategies are applied to specific words and across levels of fluency.

How Can a Real Object or Experience Be Used to Teach the Word?

Use of realia. Imagine that you are teaching vocabulary from the book, *The Tale of Peter Rabbit* by Beatrix Potter. Chamomile tea was an important part of the story. You may recall at the end of the story Peter's mother sent him to bed and gave him chamomile tea to restore him back to health. The word "chamomile" (although spelled "camomile" in the original version) poses several problems for ELLs because of its unique sound/symbol correspondence with a hard /k/ sound written as a *ch* and a silent *e* at the end.

So how can the words "chamomile tea" best be taught? If the words are taught by giving students an experience, a deeper learning takes hold. Begin by teaching "chamomile tea" with a taste of the tea (use iced tea, rather than hot, in classroom situations, with individual paper cups); tear open chamomile tea bags for the students to touch and smell. With the actual tea, the students are using multiple senses (sight, smell, taste, touch) to construct meaning of the words. Once the experience has established the meaning of chamomile tea, follow with a word card as its label.

While students are exploring the realia, record their observations on a sense chart. Make a four-column chart with the four senses. (Taste is not included because we do not want to encourage children to place objects in their mouths, particularly objects being handled by others or objects that can cause choking.)

Sense Chart for Chamomile Tea

Smell	Touch	Sight	Sound
spicy	like dry leaves	yellow/green color	only when you slurp
like chewing gum	wet and cool	like dirty water	

Providing actual experience. There are several ways of providing meaningful experiences to teach vocabulary. A walk in a park to name various shrubs and trees, or to identify bird life, is meaningful and memorable. But when teaching selected verbs, Total Physical Response (TPR) (Asher, 1982) is an ideal strategy. An effective use of TPR would be to conduct a directed drawing activity to teach the terminology of various drawing techniques, or to identify parts of face (see Chapter 3).

Asking if a word can be made meaningful with the concrete object or experience is fundamental. The first line of strategy is to look for how to use realia. If that is not possible or practical, move to the use of visuals or models.

How can a visual, or model, be used to teach the word?

Using visuals. Teaching the word *metamorphosis* takes a considerable amount of time using realia. Teachers bring a collection of moths or tadpoles to the classroom and record the physical changes the creatures go through during their life cycles. Of course the concrete experience provides the deepest level of instruction, but one can also use pictures, or a model. There are numerous picture books, card sets, and Internet resources available with sequential pictures of metamorphosis (try www.yahooligans.com for child-secure Internet pictures). I recommend the following ways in particular to use the pictures: 1) Provide multiple pictures of the same term so that students can see diverse examples. 2) Display the pictures along with the term as a semantic map in either a cluster format (surround the term with the various pictures that represent the meaning) or as a tree map (arrange the pictures below the term in a hierarchy according to subcategories). Involve the students in preparing the map by having them position and glue the pictures in relation to the core term. 3) Once students have seen pictures, have them draw their pictures of the term to be included for display. The use of display provides a continual classroom reminder of the meaning of key terms and involves the students in active construction of meaning.

Tip for parent involvement: It takes a wide range of objects, models, and pictures to make vocabulary comprehensible. Make a list of the items you need, and ask parents to help supply the items.

Using models. The use of a model is sometimes very effective for teaching vocabulary because you can teach multiple terms from a single model. For example, in geography, when teaching land forms a single model of painted papier-mâché on a cardboard base can be constructed to teach an array of terms (island, peninsula, estuary, intertidal zone, and so forth). Having small groups of students create the models for labeling and display in the classroom actively involves the students and makes the classroom come alive with meaningful representations of what the students are learning.

Use of Total Physical Response. Here is another way to use Total Physical Response to represent vocabulary. Imagine that you are listening to a lecture on the nervous system and the lecturer says the following: "Before we get to the lecture, I want to preview some of the key terms that

I will be using. In order to do this, please follow my directions. One: Hold up your hand with the fingers spread apart. This is roughly the shape of a 'dendrite.' Dendrites extend from nerve endings and attach to one another. Two: Touch your two thumbs together to imagine two dendrites connecting. This connection is called a 'synapse.' Three: Reach out to a neighbor and touch your fingers with theirs. When multiple synapses are made among several dendrites, it is called a 'ganglia.' A ganglia is a clump of nerve endings knotted together."

Notice how this strategy allows the instructor to use high-level terminology in an illustrative way without giving short shrift to the content. The use of gestures is not realia, but a representational way to understand the meaning of the words. Thinking creatively about how to apply meaningful actions and gestures can greatly serve instruction. A wonderful resource for meaningful gestures are teachers of deaf and hard-of-hearing students. Their fluency with sign language makes them skilled users of meaningful gestures.

Instructional diagrams and flowcharts for a pictorial thesaurus. Related to using pictures and creating models is having students create instructional diagrams that label key terms from a particular subject area. For example, in teaching the systems of the human body, you could use a model of the body to show each of the systems; however, if the students were divided into groups according to each system (circulatory system, gastrointestinal system, nervous system, and so forth), each group could be responsible for drawing and labeling the essential components of their assigned system to present to the class and display in the room. The value of this kind of teaching is that the students are the ones doing the work. They are making it meaningful for themselves and teaching each other content vocabulary.

Flowcharts can be helpful to show relationships and to visually outline processes. A good use of a flowchart is in comparing the words *revolution* and *evolution*. A significant difference between the two words is the flow of events over time. Revolution would be drawn as a series of events leading to a capitulation, whereas evolution would be a gradual change in adaptations over time.

Students might also create a pictorial thesaurus using a semantic map cluster on each page. A thesaurus page would include a core word at the center. Around the word would be other words with similar meanings and pictures to depict their meanings. Students might draw pictures, cut pictures from magazines or newspapers, or use computer clip art. The key is to keep it simple and to take class time to develop pages on an ongoing basis. Allow time each day to work on thesaurus pages.

A wonderful computer software tool for generating semantic maps, tree maps, instructional diagrams, and flowcharts is a program called Inspiration. There is also a program for younger children called Kidspiration. This very intuitive program allows the user to select from a large library of clip art and to arrange the pictures semantically in cluster format or in a tree map hierarchy. Pictures can also be imported from the Web or from a scanner. The tool has several amazing features. While students are selecting pictures and arranging them on the screen, the labels for the pictures are placed automatically on the screen. Further, the program is designed to generate a linear outline of the semantic map. It also allows the user to insert notes that are placed in the auto-generated outline (see Appendix for directions).

Is the Word Conceptual or Abstract? Use Unpacking Strategies

Vocabulary that is abstract poses special challenges to teaching ELLs. I use the term "unpacking" in reference to teaching abstract words because their meaning is not readily apparent, or cannot be represented by realia or a visual. Before meaningful instruction can take place a teacher must do some background work. There are a number of strategies that will help make words meaningful; but nothing replaces knowing the word thoroughly. This may sound unnecessary to emphasize, but let me illustrate with a common word that we all use.

The word *color* is easy to recognize, but surprisingly complex to define. Color can be defined as a range of hue, value, and intensity. Hue is a continuum of colors related to temperatures from cold to hot, value a continuum from light to dark, and intensity a continuum from bright to dull. These continua are also referred to as spectra. Of course, this does not deal with the concept of primary, secondary, and tertiary colors. The point is that some words pack multiple meanings which need to be "unpacked" before teaching can occur. To teach color without exploring hue, value, and intensity does not do justice to understanding the word. Knowing the word requires developing background knowledge. The first place to go for background knowledge is to check the word's etymology.

Check the etymology. Etymology is the study of word origins. There are several reasons for studying a word's etymology. Knowing an etymology tells the story of a word. It reminds us that words are organic rather than fixed, that words change over time, and that they are used for a variety of intentions. Studying etymology exposes a word's roots and derivations. Etymologies also get to the grounded meaning of a word which often provides a visual for teaching the word.

Look at the word *spirit*, for example. After studying its etymology, one sees that the word's original meaning is "breath"; it has the same root as the words "respiration," re-breathing, and "conspiracy," a kind of breathing or whispering together. Knowing the root and related meaning of "spirit" as breathing dictates a simple shared experience in teaching the word's meaning. The teacher might simply have students experience breathing as a way to begin to understand and remember "spirit."

At times, studying etymologies can seem like being a detective uncovering the truth about a word. Any quality dictionary will supply etymologies; but it may require some digging to find the meaning of root words. Several Internet resources are of great help in studying etymologies. One free resource is www.dictionary.com. A paid subscriber resource is from the Oxford English Dictionary, www.oed.com. Web-based resources make finding etymologies tremendously easy and a task that students at the intermediate level of fluency and above can do for themselves with relative ease.

Explore related roots. Related to researching etymologies is looking at related words in order to get to a grounded understanding of a word's meaning. When one looks at a range of words that share the same root meaning, it reinforces the meaning of the word in question. This can be illustrated by looking at words related to the word *static*, as in static electricity. The meaning of *static* may not be readily apparent. However, if you ask a group of students to find other words that begin with *sta-*, the meaning comes to light. Although there are numerous words beginning with *sta-*, you can expect students to suggest common words such as stay, stand, station.

Static electricity, in other words, is the kind of electricity that stays, stands, or stations itself on the surface of an object. Exploring related roots provides visual insight into the word's meaning. A picture of static can now be formed, whereas before looking at related roots, the word appeared to be more abstract.

Use of cognates. Once when I was working with a group of Khmer-speaking Cambodian students, I was surprised to learn that the Khmer word for whale is *baleen*. The Spanish word for whale is *ballena*. In English, we refer to baleen whales as those without teeth, that use long strands of baleen to literally strain the water out of their catch of tiny krill to eat. Obviously, the word is an example of a cognate from Romance language roots. Although Khmer is not a Romance language, it acquired the word, one would suspect, several centuries ago when European whalers sailed into port. One would not expect English to share cognates with an Asian language; in this case, however, a cognate is like a bridge or touch point between the two languages.

Tip for parent involvement: Parents can help identify cognates. Ask them to highlight words in the English text that are similar in Spanish. In the classroom, create a cognate word wall based on the highlighted words found by the parents.

It takes specialized knowledge of languages to use cognates. Knowing when a word is a cognate is important. Some words that are spelled similarly may not share the same meaning; these are called false cognates. Spanish shares many cognates with English and is a language that is used by a great number of students in our schools. Rodriguez (2001) has provided some insights into using cognates with Spanish. Tables 5.1 and 5.2 can help understand the nature of Spanish cognates and which ones can be readily applied to instruction.

Primary Language Support

Although it appears counterintuitive at first glance, using a student's primary language (home language) as a means to introduce vocabulary and content instruction is a very efficient way to teach English. A simple yet effective way to provide primary language support is called preview/review (Lessow-Hurley, 1990).

Have you ever found yourself in the following situation? You are in the middle of teaching a lesson. You think you are making perfect sense; but then, you suddenly realize that the class is staring at you blankly. The students had quit following what you were saying about five minutes earlier, but did not stop to tell you so. In the middle of the lesson, then, you halt, back up, and define key terms and review main points for the class. All at once you hear the group say, "Oh, so that's what you're talking about."

There are a number of reasons why the above scenario takes place. One is that key terms and essential concepts were not previewed prior to presenting the body of instruction, or that key terms were not meaningful to the students when they were being previewed. Another possible reason is that the key terms were so new and unfamiliar that the students promptly forgot what they meant.

TABLE 5.1   *Spanish Cognates*

Type	Identical Cognates	Similar Spelling Cognates	Spelling Less Apparent	Oral Cognates	Partial Meaning Cognate	Root Cognates	False Cognates
English	fatal hotel actor	contamination evidence castigate	sport perilous	pleasure peace	letter (alphabet, correspondence)	disappear appear	bigot embarrassed
Spanish	*fatal hotel actor*	*contaminación evidencia castigar*	*deporte peligroso*	*placer paz*	*letra, carta*	*desaparecer aparecer*	*bigote (moustache) embarazada (pregnant)*

Source: T. A. Rodrgriguez (2001). "Teaching ideas: From the known to the unknown: Using cognates to teach English to Spanish literates." *Reading Teacher 54* (8), 744–746.

TABLE 5.2 *Other Common Cognates*

English	Spanish	English	Spanish
Writing		*Book Terms*	
alphabet	*alfabeto*	appendix	*apéndice*
punctuation	*puntuación*	atlas	*atlas*
initials	*initials*	volume	*volumen*
letter	*letra*	page	*página*
symbol	*símbolo*	introduction	*introducción*
comma	*coma*	title	*título*
Math		*Science*	
decimal	*decimal*	hypothesis	*hipótesis*
double	*doble*	acid	*ácido*
fraction	*fracción*	metal	*metal*
dozen	*docena*	ozone	*ozono*
circle	*círculo*	corrosion	*corrosión*
equal	*igual*	plastics	*plásticos*
History		*Animals*	
civilization	*civilización*	animal(s)	*animal(es)*
history	*historia*	human	*humano*
past	*pasado*	kangaroo	*canguro*
pioneer	*pionero*	elephant	*elefante*
colonial	*colonial*	dinosaur	*dinosaurio*
diary	*diario*	eagle	*águila*
Common Words		*Your Own List*	
action	*acción*		
group	*grupo*		
program	*programa*		
opportunity	*oportunidad*		
popular	*popular*		
family	*familia*		

Source: R. Nash (1997). *NTC's dictionary of Spanish cognates.* Chicago: NTC Publishing Group.

Meaningfully previewing key vocabulary and essential content is an effective way to conduct instruction. Previewing vocabulary and essential content in the student's primary language can be even more effective, ensuring greater understanding for teaching the lesson in English. Once students have a grasp of the meaning of key vocabulary, a working knowledge of their usage, and an outline of essential concepts in their own language, the lesson in English can flow without being interrupted at midpoint by lengthy explanations of misunderstood words or ideas. Finishing a lesson with a brief review of the key terms and essential content in the primary language reinforces the meaning. To take it a step further, use the review time at the end of the lesson to engage students in primary-language discussions about their learning. Ask students to paraphrase the learning in their own words and raise questions that they were unable to formulate in English.

Preview/review actually creates language zones in classroom instruction. The key for the teacher is to teach as a language model. In the preview section, the teacher is a Spanish model on proper use and pronunciation of the vocabulary while also providing a logical sequence of the lesson. Then, the teacher switches to English instruction to create, in effect, an English zone where English is maintained as a model. Even though students may raise questions or have comments in another language, the teacher maintains English as a model of conventional usage. This requires mental discipline on the part of the teacher. The teacher does not discourage the use of another language, but remains a model for proper use of English. Often, the teacher will rephrase a student's question or comment using conventional English as part of a language teaching strategy. At the end of the lesson, the language zone shifts back to the primary language for review and discussion.

Tip for parent involvement: If you are literate in the child's home language, extend the concept of preview/review to the home. Provide an advanced organizer for content instruction in the home language at the beginning of the week with instructions to review the essential lesson concepts and vocabulary. Follow up with a homework assignment to discuss the learning and vocabulary with family members later on in the week.

The use of preview/review raises frequently asked questions (FAQs). The following are some FAQs about preview/review.

What if the teacher does not speak the students' primary language? It takes a highly qualified teacher who is literate in the students' primary language to expertly use preview/review; however, some teachers are fortunate to work with bilingual teacher aides who can provide preview/review for the class while the teacher teaches the body of the lesson in English. In some cases, peer tutors can help provide preview/review instruction.

What if the administration does not allow anything but English instruction? Know the education code for your state and district. Go to your administrator for authorization and be sure you know the policies prior to using another language for instruction. It is also important to inform parents about your classroom practice. Invite them to observe the quality of your instruction. Dual-language instruction has a controversial history. Although preview/review pedagogically is a highly sound instructional practice, it may not be perceived that way by uninformed individuals. Therefore, be advised to employ primary-language support within your educational system's guidelines in consultation with knowledgeable practitioners.

What if there are multiple languages in the classroom? Preview/review was designed to work in a classroom setting with two languages, although variations can be made to accommodate other languages. Pairing students according to language groups can facilitate using preview/review. If students have access to dual-language dictionaries in their own primary language and English, they can look up words prior to instruction. The teacher can preview the terms and then ask students to paraphrase the vocabulary definitions and lesson outline in their own words. After instruction in English, they can review the instruction in the primary language as well.

Use Similes and Metaphorical Thinking with Word Study Charts

Another strategy for exploring the meaning of words that do not initially lend themselves to realia or showing a visual is to apply similes and metaphorical thinking with word study charts. A simple way to initiate similes and metaphorical thinking is to ask, "What do you think it is like?" Earlier in the chapter, I referred to the word *brilliant*. Again let me raise the question: What is "brilliant" like? There are two directions to go with this word: one is the realm of light and brightness; the other is the realm of intelligence and genius. To illustrate those realms of meaning, make a semantic map that includes pictures and words arranged around the core word, showing on one side brightness and on the other side intelligence. Include questions on the chart such as, What is "brilliant" like? What are examples of "brilliant" around us?

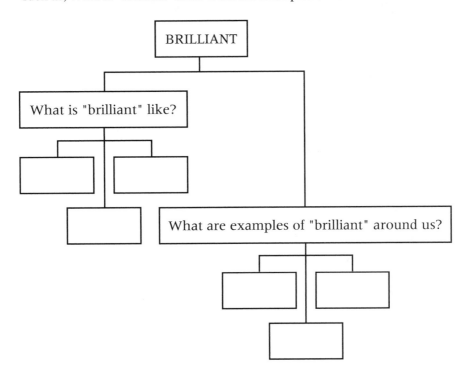

Tip for parent involvement: Send home a word study chart that is partially complete. Ask parents to help find magazine or newspaper pictures to complete the chart.

Developing Fluency

Understanding the meaning of vocabulary words is vital to learning. Students also need to put the words to use immediately in order to develop fluency with the terms. Developing fluency has several benefits. Fluent use of a new word ensures retention of the word in the future and in other contexts. Embedding fluency development in the lesson also provides a check for conventional usage, pronunciation, and spelling. The following section shows how to develop fluency with interactive games, digital flash cards, and developing descriptive vocabulary.

Interactive Games to Develop Fluency with New Vocabulary

One of the easiest ways to embed fluency development in a lesson is to play a game. The higher the level of social interaction in the game, the greater the opportunity to use the word multiple times, which results in fluency development. The following is a list of games with simple directions that are highly interactive and provide students with practice of new terminology to develop fluency.

Tip for parent involvement: Send word cards home with children along with directions for a specific fluency game. Families can play the games at home and reinforce vocabulary development.

1. **Sentence line-ups**

    *   Provide a variety of word cards color coded and organized according to nouns, verbs, adjectives, adverbs, prepositions, and articles (one to two cards per student).

    *   Form small groups.

    *   Ask students to form coherent sentences about a specific topic by lining up the word cards.

    *   The rest of the class must read the sentence line-up.

2. **Who am I? Or What am I?**

    *   Tape a name card or word card to the back of each student.

    *   Given a set amount of time (three to five minutes), the students must ask yes/no questions to find out who or what the card represents.

3. **Concentration**

    *   Make up a set of card pairs, each matching a word to a picture.

    *   Place all cards in an array facedown on a table.

    *   Students must match a picture card to a word card in order to obtain points.

    *   The student with the most paired cards wins.

4. **Adaptation of the Dictionary game**

    *   Use key vocabulary words.

    *   Divide students into teams.

    *   One student will have the correct definition, others will have to make up a plausible definition to bluff opponents.

    *   Team that guesses the correct definition receives a point.

5. **Charades**

    *   Using key vocabulary, ask one or more students to act out a word.

    *   Other students must guess what word is being acted out.

6. **Adaptation of picture definition game**

    *   Students are asked to draw a picture representing a key vocabulary word.

    *   Other students try to guess what word is being drawn.

    *   May be played in teams or pairs.

7. Crossword puzzles (Avoid solitary work. Have students work in pairs.)

- Have students make their own crossword puzzles, using quarter-inch-square grid paper.

- Tell students to input key vocabulary words.

- They may try out the crossword puzzles on each other.

Developing Descriptive Vocabulary

A significant way to foster encountering meaning is to develop descriptive vocabulary. Think about how a wine connoisseur describes wine. At first it appears that the taster has a vivid imagination with descriptions of "herbaceous" or "fruity." What really is at play is the setting of two descriptors against each other at opposite ends of a continuum. Some examples are sweet versus sour or weak versus strong. The use of a continuum to clarify descriptions is directly applicable to teaching students how to articulate their own perceptions of experience. Here are some continua that are simple and can be used to help students describe words or experiences.

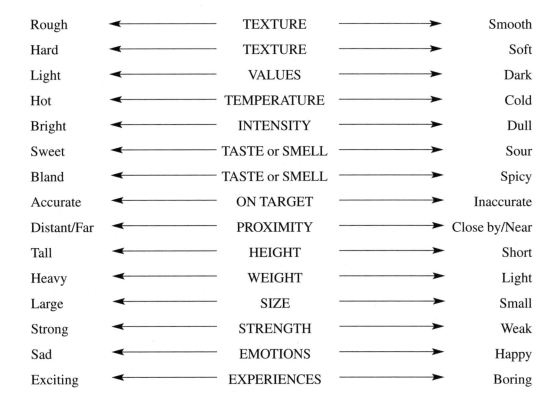

Rough	TEXTURE	Smooth
Hard	TEXTURE	Soft
Light	VALUES	Dark
Hot	TEMPERATURE	Cold
Bright	INTENSITY	Dull
Sweet	TASTE or SMELL	Sour
Bland	TASTE or SMELL	Spicy
Accurate	ON TARGET	Inaccurate
Distant/Far	PROXIMITY	Close by/Near
Tall	HEIGHT	Short
Heavy	WEIGHT	Light
Large	SIZE	Small
Strong	STRENGTH	Weak
Sad	EMOTIONS	Happy
Exciting	EXPERIENCES	Boring

If you insert graded words into each continuum, such as "very/highly" or "a little/somewhat," you add range to the descriptors. Now you can describe a wide variety of items with appropriate descriptors such as "highly accurate" or "somewhat inaccurate," "very rough" or "a little rough." By displaying these terms on a chart in the classroom, students have a quick reference for making appropriate descriptions. Descriptive continua can be applied across the curriculum in the following ways: Literary Analysis: character study; Math/Statistics: describing a frequency table; Science: describing experimental phenomena.

Appendix: Helpful Computer Software: Web Building with Inspiration

Getting Started with Inspiration

(See www.Inspiration.com for a free trial version)
Toolbar

Outline:	Generates an outline of your tree chart diagram.
New Look:	Previews default picture/symbols for the diagram.
Rapid Fire:	Shortcut to entering extensive ideas related to a symbol.
Link:	Creates a link between symbols displayed by an arrow.
Add Note:	Creates a text box for additional information related to a symbol.
Create:	Positions a new symbol in either a horizontal, vertical, or diagonal direction.
Position:	Used to grasp and move the entire diagram.
Arrange:	Provides a variety of display formats for the diagram.
Spell:	Checks spelling.
Library Box:	Displays a wide range of pictorial libraries to use to make symbols. (Left/right arrows shuttle through libraries; down arrow displays available topics.)

Task #1: The Main Idea Symbol

1. The program opens with a "Main Idea" symbol. This is the starting point and cannot be deleted.
2. Double-click on the symbol. In the text box below the icon, highlight "Main Idea" and write over it the word "Weather."
3. Click the down arrow in the library box. Select "Science." Select "Weather."
4. At the top of the weather library, choose a text box symbol (oval, shadow box, rounded corner box, basic box, cloud, or off-set box). Click on your choice.
5. The symbol you have selected is now the main idea "Weather" symbol in your diagram.
6. Click once on the symbol to highlight it. Highlighting is noted by a red square surrounding the symbol.
7. Click and hold down the mouse button, and drag a corner of the red box to size your symbol.

Task #2: Create a Diagram

1. Click once on the main idea "Weather" symbol.
2. Move the cursor to the tool bar button, "Create"—refrain from clicking.
3. Note that the arrows light up blue to designate the position of a new symbol in a horizontal, vertical, or diagonal direction. Each time you want to create a new symbol, decide the position of the new symbol, then click on the "Create" button.
4. Click once on the main idea symbol each time you wish to create a new related symbol.
5. Repeat the process with each new symbol.
6. Create four new symbols linked to and surrounding the main idea "Weather" symbol.
7. Click on a new symbol once. Select a picture from the weather library to represent your idea. Repeat the process until each new symbol has a unique picture displayed.
8. Double-click on each new symbol to write in the white box the label for that symbol.
9. You may also wish to click and drag a symbol to reposition it.

Task #3: Add Notes/Rapid Fire

1. Click once on a new symbol surrounding the main idea.
2. On the toolbar, select "Add Notes" and a text box will appear.
3. Write a more detailed explanation of your symbol.
4. Click on the background to close the note.
5. You may also click on "Rapid Fire" as a shortcut to adding information to a symbol.
6. The information that you have written appears in the outline.

Task #4: Automatic Outlining

1. Select the "Outline" button on the tool bar.
2. Your diagram is automatically outlined.
3. You may even change the order of your outline by simply clicking and dragging the outline statement to the position you choose.
4. Return to the diagram by selecting the "Diagram" button on the tool bar.

Task #5: Arranging a Tree Chart

1. Select the "Arrange" button on the tool bar. A menu box will appear with a variety of diagram arrangements to choose from.

2. Pick a new arrangement for your diagram. Click on "OK."

3. View your new diagram arrangement.

References

Chamot, A., & O'Mally, J. (1987). The cognitive academic language learning approach: A bridge to the mainstream. *TESOL Quarterly, 21,* 227–249.

Dewey, J. (1902). *The child and the curriculum.* Chicago, IL: University of Chicago Press.

Lessow-Hurley, J. (1990). *The foundations of dual language instruction.* White Plains, NY: Longman.

Nash, R. (1997). *NTC's dictionary of Spanish cognates.* Chicago, IL: NTC Publishing Group.

Piaget, J. (1926). *The language and thought of a child.* New York: Harcourt, Brace and World.

Rodgriguez, T. A. (2001). "Teaching ideas: From the known to the unknown: Using cognates to teach English to Spanish literates." *Reading Teacher 54*(8), 744–746.

6

Supporting Reading Instruction

TESOL Goals and Standards

Goal 1: To use English to communicate in social settings

Standard 3: Students will use learning strategies to extend their communicative competence

Goal 2: To use English to achieve academically in all content areas

Standard 1: Students will use English to interact in the classroom

Standard 2: Students will use English to obtain, process, construct, and provide subject matter information in spoken and written form

Standard 3: Students will use appropriate learning strategies to construct and apply academic knowledge

Reading in the Long Run

In a review of effective reading programs for ELLs, Slavin and Cheung (2003) found that many of the same components in comprehensive reading programs for English-only speakers were helpful for Spanish bilingual students. Evidence from the reviewed studies also favored high-quality programs that used bilingual approaches for reading instruction. This concurs with other research evidence that found children's reading proficiency in their first language to be a strong predictor of reading performance in English (Garcia, 2000; Reese, Garnier, Gallimore, & Goldenberg, 2000). Although establishing a bilingual reading program at a school site is beyond the scope of this book, the practice is highly recommended. The strategies and activities found in this chapter work with both English-only and ELL students. What is unique is that the strategies and activities are differentiated to match the level of the reader.

I use the phrase "reading in the long run" because, as a long-distance runner, I find certain parallels between running and reading. They are tasks for both purpose and pleasure. They require regular practice to develop proficiency. For some, the task is easier to perform than for others. But one does not need to be the fastest to get enjoyment out of the activity.

Other specific parallels exist between running and reading that give insight into generating lifelong readers. These parallels are warming up, rhythm/fluency, strength training/word power, speed and pacing, visualizing/imagining, independent/shared activity, developing a love for the task, and recording progress. All these contribute to persistence and focus for the long run. Let's look more closely at the parallels.

Warming Up

Just as with running, reading benefits from warm-up activities. There are many ways to warm up to reading. For the purposes of this book, we will look at five different ways and how they vary across levels of fluency for ELLs. Be reminded that a teacher would only use one of the warm-up strategies a day. Trying to do several warm-up strategies at a time would risk frustrating the reader. Also keep in mind that a warm-up activity should not take longer than five to ten minutes.

> ***Tip for parent involvement:*** Demonstrate to parents how to walk through a book prior to reading. Show how to hold the book while reading so that all can see. Teach parents to ask predicting questions as they read to their children.

Book walks. There are essentially four elements to a book walk: book orientation, predicting questions, story overview, and highlights. Let's look at how to address these across levels of fluency. There is very little difference in how one would approach a book walk for early intermediate to intermediate and early advanced to advanced, so those levels are grouped together in two headings (see Table 6.1).

TABLE 6.1 *Book Walks*

	Beginning	*Early Intermediate and Intermediate*	*Early Advanced and Advanced*
Book Orientation	• Preview front/back cover art • Identify title • Identify author and illustrator (show pictures obtained from author's Web site)	(Same as prior level) • Note publisher, date • Dedication • Note author and illustrator information on overleaf	(Same as prior level) • Review Library of Congress information
Predicting Questions	• Ask yes/no questions: "Do you think that this will happen next?" • Call for gestures: "Point to the next action." • Draw a picture of what you think will happen next	• Ask either/or questions: "How will Peter escape? By losing his jacket or by tearing off a button?" • Ask open-ended questions: "What do you think will happen next?" • Tell your neighbor what will happen	• Think of two possible actions that could happen • Discuss your ideas with your neighbor • Summarize what your neighbor thought might happen • Write down the best possible outcome from those you've discussed
Story Overview	• Conduct a picture walk through the story • Identify settings, characters, and events • Provide a pictorial storyboard to order events	(Same as prior level) • Summarize the main events of the story • Use a graphic organizer to map the story events	(Same as prior level) • Outline story events • Create your own flowchart of story events

(*continued*)

TABLE 6.1   (Continued)

	Beginning	*Early Intermediate and Intermediate*	*Early Advanced and Advanced*
Highlights	• Read a selection of a favorite part • Point to your favorite part of the story • Note other books by the same author for free reading at another time	(Same as prior level) • Tell your neighbor about your favorite part of the story • Note descriptive text of setting, characters, events	(Same as prior level) • Create a digital book walk for other students using presentation software (*See end of chapter for details.*)

Context development. Warming up to read means giving students background information. Depending on the story selection, the context development may vary. Five areas of context development are other stories by the same author, geographical location, historical setting, key aspects of the story, and character traits and motivations. How you approach these across fluency levels is relatively consistent. A key strategy is to make the process as visual as possible. Web-based graphics are essential to developing context. Web sites like www.yahooligans.com are very helpful as well as the author's personal website (see Table 6.2).

TABLE 6.2   *Context Development*

	Beginning	*Early Intermediate and Intermediate*	*Early Advanced and Advanced*
Other stories by the same author	• Display an array of books by the same author • Preview each book • Make them available for free reading	• Identify and describe settings, events, and characters from other stories by the same author	• Identify other authors with similar stories • Compare and contrast settings, events, and characters from other stories by other authors
Geographical location and/or interior settings	• Provide pictures of the location • Locate setting on a pictorial map • Use play furniture to arrange interior settings	• Trace events on a map • Picture search the geographical location • Draw room arrangements for interior settings	• Conduct Internet research of geographical location
Historical setting	• Display pictures that depict the time period of the story • Note clothing, architecture, transportation, etc.	• Note key events of the time period that influence the events of the story	• Find newspaper articles from the time period via the Internet • Identify major events of the day • Discuss changes over time
Key aspects of the story	• Show pictures of the story's climax • Identify major events in the story	• Create a story ladder of events leading to a climax	• Identify cause and effect of major events in the story • Use a highlighter to mark key events in a story

Character traits and/or motivations	• Make a semantic map of random traits of a selectedmain character	• Order random character traits into a tree map organizer	• Identify flat characters who do not change • Identify protagonist(s) and antagonist(s) • Discuss character motivations

Mini-Lessons. Mini-lesson formats fit nicely with the warm-up metaphor for reading instruction. Taking a few minutes for instruction of key vocabulary, word analysis, grammar/punctuation conventions, story grammar, or genre will help the ELL read through difficult passages and increase comprehension. Note the difference between vocabulary development and word analysis. Vocabulary development focuses primarily on meaning whereas word analysis attends to linguistic features of words. Similarly, note that grammar/punctuation conventions refers to grammatical features of sentences, paragraphs, punctuation marks and so forth, while story grammar refers to the structure of a type of story. Table 6.3 describes what to do for each level of fluency.

Tip for parent involvement: Encourage parents to share with their children their own experiences that have a connection with the story. For example, if the story is set on the coast, share prior experiences at the beach.

TABLE 6.3 *Mini-lessons*

	Beginning	*Early Intermediate and Intermediate*	*Early Advanced and Advanced*
Key Vocabulary	• For verbs, use meaningful actions (see Total Physical Response in Chapter 3) • For nouns, use realia, visuals, models • Create a thesaurus with pictures labeled • Display a pictorial word bank on a wall chart • Explain meanings of words in the students' primary language	• Create a personal thesaurus with a key word at the center of a semantic cluster map of other words with similar meanings (see directions below under Strength Training/ Word Power) • Highlight key words when they appear in the story	• Look up words using an Internet source such as www.dictionary.com
Word Analysis	• Identify letters in initial, medial, and final position • Identify letter-sound correspondence • Segment words into syllables • Identify consonant blends • Note function of certain words as "helping words," "sight words," etc.	• Arrange words in family groups (-ar, -er, -ir, -or, -ur) • Analyze vowel digraphs • Note homophones and homographs • Build words with roots, prefixes, infixes, suffixes • Analyze inflected endings (-ed, -s, -ing) • Analyze contractions	• Trace word origins • Study root meanings • Compare multiple meanings • Identify use of slang and idiomatic expressions • Study cultural influences on words • Identify Latin, Greek, Middle English, etc. roots

(continued)

TABLE 6.3   (Continued)

	Beginning	*Early Intermediate and Intermediate*	*Early Advanced and Advanced*
Grammar/ Punctuation Conventions	• Syntax: Use word cards to create sentence line-ups of selected sentences • Identify ending punctuation • Note paragraph indents	• Parts of speech: color code words as nouns, adjectives, adverbs • Compose Cinquain poetry • Identify unique constructions in a story • Build sentences with parts of speech • Introduce use and function of quotation marks, comma, semicolon, colon	• Compare selected sentences used in story texts • Diagram sentences • Peer editing
Story Grammar	• Identify beginning, middle, and end of story • Describe setting and characters • Identify problem/solution	• Identify and describe story elements: conflict, key events, climax, denouement • Highlight shifts in the storyline • Create a wall chart of similar stories to detail setting, characters, problem/solution	• Compare conflict, key events, climax, and denouement with similar stories • Outline the story
Genre	• Identify fiction versus nonfiction	• Study unique features of each genre category • Sort and label stories according to appropriate genre	• Compare key features of selected stories that place them in certain genres

Responding to reading. Literary response occurs involuntarily when one is reading a story. Readers cannot help but picture events or feel emotion evoked by a good story. Responding to reading can be an individual experience or shared. Shared experiences give insight into the way a reader perceives and interprets the meaning of the story. Cultural nuance and individual difference in understanding can be explored with literary response. Table 6.4 shows ways to respond to reading individually and as a shared experience according to levels of fluency.

TABLE 6.4   *Responding to Reading*

	Beginning	*Early Intermediate and Intermediate*	*Early Advanced and Advanced*
Individual Experience	• Draw a picture of a favorite part of the story • Describe the picture to a literate adult to transcribe in a journal • Draw yourself into the story (Where are you? Who are you? What are you doing?)	• Write about your favorite part of the story in a journal • Picture yourself at various places in the story (outside as a spectator, next door as a neighbor, side by side as a friend, as the main character)	• Maintain a two-column journal. Cite special sections in the left column and write responses in the right column.

Shared Experience

- Listen to a proficient reader read the story
- Use a face chart showing a range of emotions to identify how the story made the student feel
- Create a chart story in asmall group
- Illustrate the chart story
- Copy the chart story in a journal

- Discuss the following questions: "What did you see in your mind as you read the story? If you were the main character, how would you feel?"
- Collaborate with a partner to compose a description of what was visualized by reading the story

- Write a review/critique of the in your mind as you read the story to publish in a classroom newsletter
- Compose poetry or songs in response to the story

Tip for parent involvement: Practice asking questions about stories, such as the following:
• What were you thinking as you read the story?
• Have you ever felt like the character?
• What would you do if you were in that situation?
• How would you change the story?
Even parents who are illiterate can ask these questions as they listen to their child read and discuss the story.

Rhythm/Fluency

Developing rhythm and pacing in running parallels fluency in reading in that they both require practice on a regular basis. Running is only developed by getting out and running. You can look at videos about running, study form, and plan a running schedule; but without stepping out on the track or the road, one cannot develop the rhythm to have stamina to run. This does not mean running hard every day, though, which leads to burnout and injury. It means running easy some days, fast on other days, long on other days, with warm-ups and speed and strength training inserted. A running program would build to a point each week for a long run. The distance and the time for each session would progressively increase by 1 to 5 percent increments, and the location and terrain for each run would vary. A simplistic version of a regular running program would look something like the following:

Day 1: Warm-up/Very easy run/Strength training
Day 2: Warm-up/Easy run
Day 3: Warm-up/Tempo training
Day 4: Warm-up/Easy run
Day 5: Long, slowly paced run (no need for warm-up due to the slow pace)
Day 6: Rest
Day 7: Warm-up/Easy run

Now, think of a weekly classroom reading program that asks students to read at a variety of levels, times, and durations with vocabulary development built in and even a rest day once a week. Just as with running, a warm-up time is provided. But with reading, the warm-up would take various forms to preview the reading or highlight certain aspects of reading. Picture a weekly classroom reading program like this:

Day 1: Warm-up (book walk)/Easy read/Vocabulary development for word power
Day 2: Warm-up (context development)/Normal reading
Day 3: Warm-up (mini-lessons/word analysis)/Tempo reading for fluency training
Day 4: Warm-up (vocabulary check)/Normal reading
Day 5: Long read (extended continuous read time for 30 minutes or more)/Literary response
Day 6: Rest
Day 7: Warm-up (reader responses)/Easy read

Each week the length of reading time would be increased by a few minutes and the warm-up activities would vary to meet the observed needs of the students. Now let's break down each component according to levels of English language proficiency. For example, the way an advanced ELL would warm up with a book walk would vary from the way a book walk would be conducted with a beginning-level ELL.

Tip for parent involvement: Ask parents to have their child read a short story or poem several times to develop fluency.

Strength Training/Word Power

Strength training in running parallels word power in reading. The primary way to develop vocabulary is through reading. There are a number of strategies to develop vocabulary. Many of these are addressed in Chapter 5; however, the following are strategies that empower the students to develop vocabulary knowledge for themselves. The first strategy is to initiate a personal thesaurus. The second is to use Web-based resources.

A personal thesaurus. One would think that a student should first initiate a personal dictionary; however, a thesaurus can provide the definition function of a dictionary while being more flexible and easier to develop and maintain.

- Start the personal thesaurus with a loose-leaf binder and several pages of paper.
- In the center of each page, draw a diagram of a cluster map, sometimes called a word web. (A cluster map is basically a circle with branches reaching out from the center like wagon-wheel spokes.)
- Write a generative word in the center of each of the clusters. (Use key vocabulary words from your reading selection.)
- As students encounter a word with a similar meaning to the word in the center, they can add it to the cluster by writing it at the end of one of the branches.
- When appropriate, include a drawing of the key word or one of the branched-off words.
- Add a page each time you want to include a new key word.
- Encourage students to add key words to their thesaurus.
- As a spelling activity, students can take spelling lists and include the words in their thesaurus. This requires them to think if the word is an alternate meaning of a key word already included or if they need to start a new page.
- Review each thesaurus on a periodic basis (once a week or every other week).

If students have access to individual computers, they can develop a personal thesaurus using Inspiration software (www.Inspiration.com). This intuitive program fosters creating word webs and includes an extensive clip art library that lets the user illustrate each word.

Web-based resources. Although there are numerous sites available, the following two sites have proven to be extremely helpful particularly for vocabulary development.

An easily accessible resource that includes a variety of useful tools is www.dictionary.com. It combines a number of search engines for words, including words in other languages such as Spanish, German, or French. A given word search provides a pronunciation key, a brief etymology, and multiple definitions. It also includes links to other dictionary programs and search engines.

An excellent child-protected search engine that provides educational resources across subject areas is www.yahooligans.com. It is a wonderful resource for pictures as well as educational text material.

Tempo and Pacing/Fluency

Although it is important, speed is not the primary goal of reading. Sure there remain speed-reading courses on the market, but reading in the long run, for information or pleasure, is more a matter of reading at an appropriate pace that allows for clear comprehension. (Imagine comparing speed reading to "speed watching." Given a prescribed speed-watching course you can watch five movies in only forty-five minutes. Speed becomes ludicrous in such a scenario.) Fluency is a more appropriate way to express this idea. Fluency does involve the speed and pacing that the reader adopts. More efficient readers tend to read at a more rapid rate when appropriate. More efficient readers do several tasks as they read. They preview what they are about to read, and they do not read word for word but read groups of meaningful word clusters. They also read regularly and they reread. The following are strategies to enhance fluency. Some involve speed, others pacing; but ultimately, fluency is dictated by comprehension at an appropriate rate.

Digital flash cards (Part 1). Use presentation software to practice high-frequency words. Here's an idea to improve upon the old flash card concept. Use media presentation software like Power-Point to create flash cards for high-frequency words. (Instructions for using PowerPoint are given at the end of this chapter.) Select a two-column slide and type in the high-frequency words you wish to have students practice. Type in four words in each column for a total of eight words on a slide. Then animate the words to appear in a sequential order. You can use the "Rehearse Timings" menu option to adjust the duration of time each word appears. In a short period of time, you can create a wide range of slides that provide students with practice in reading key words fluently. For fun, finish with applause from the auditory menu options.

Digital flash cards (Part 2). Use presentation software to practice reading meaningful clusters of words at a glance. Based on the same idea as above, create a PowerPoint presentation that shows in succession noun phrases and verb phrases. This will give the students individual practice in looking for meaning in sets of words as opposed to reading word for word.

Repetitive reading for time. Each week give the students a selected text to read and reread for practice. For the first read-through, ask the students to select a partner to time how long it takes to read the text completely. Record the first reading time on a table (see below). Then have students take time each day, in class and/or at home, to read through the same selection. The repetition is for practice to increase speed. After having practiced reading for a week, time the reading selection again and record the difference. Keep track on a graph of the difference in time between the first and the final read-through.

Reading Times	*Week 1*			*Week 2*			*Week 3*			*Week 4*		
Student Name	1st	2nd	Δ*	1st	2nd	Δ	1st	2nd	Δ	1st	2nd	Δ

*The triangle symbol Δ, the Greek letter *delta*, signifies change—the difference in the times from the first to the second reading.

Tip for parent involvement: Once students learn how to use and read the above table, they can use it at home to track the difference in reading times.

Visualizing/Imagining

Competitive runners take time to visualize and imagine prior to running. They picture the course layout in their minds, and also imagine themselves running at various paces throughout the course. They even imagine the winning moment of breaking the tape at the end of the race. Visualizing and imagining are characteristic strategies of skilled readers as well. Visualizing and imagining contribute to increased comprehension and retention (Sadoski & Quast, 1990).

Visualizing and imagining are two different processes. For the purpose of clarity, *visualizing* is defined as a form of picturing the events of a story in one's mind. *Imagining* is defined as a way to explore one's unique perceptions while reading a story (see Table 6.5).

Graphic organizers. Graphic organizers have been shown to be useful tools for visualizing story events (Reutzel & Cooter, 2004; Gordon & Braun, 1983). Consider readers visualizing the layout of a story using a pictorial story ladder. Usually story ladders are developed only on a verbal level. A strategy to increase comprehension across levels of fluency is to represent the actions and events of the story in picture form. Have students collaborate to create a wall-sized, pictorial story ladder. Pairs of students draw selected scenes from a story that lead to a climax and the resulting events of the denouement. Then as a group, they arrange the pictures they draw in a ladder format. Use the following graphic organizer to generate a pictorial story ladder. The pictures are mounted on a bulletin board and connected with yarn or colored string.

Students from beginning to advanced levels of fluency can participate in this activity. To facilitate increased comprehension, pair students heterogeneously. By pairing a beginning-level student with an intermediate- or advanced-level student, the higher-level student can more easily refer back to the text to assist the beginner.

Imagining is a different kind of activity; it is more idiosyncratic. To foster imagining, provide ways for students to think creatively about the story. Give them ways to express their own reflections, how they perceive characters, and what they picture in their minds.

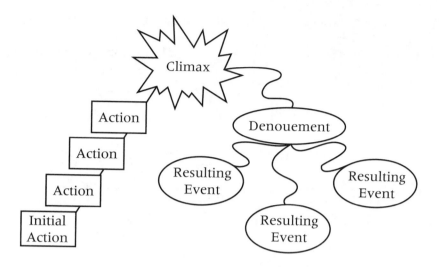

This kind of reflective work requires aesthetic questions, illustrative journals, and guided imagery.

Aesthetic questions. Aesthetic questions call on the reader to explore what they are thinking as they read, how they feel, how they would change the story. Cox (2004) has developed a series of aesthetic questions based on the reader response theory work of Rosenblatt (1978). Beyond asking questions to recall information about a story, aesthetic questions elicit evocations from a literary work. Following are suggested aesthetic questions to evoke imagining:

> What were you thinking as you read the story?
> How did you feel when _____ happened?
> Which characters are you drawn to? Why?
> If you were one of the characters, which would you be? Why?
> What would you change if you were in the story?
> What do you see in your mind when you read these words?
> Does this remind you of any other stories? Which ones? Why?

The above questions are open-ended and will not be appropriate for a beginning-level ELL. Following are some adaptations that can be made to include beginning-level students:

> Draw your favorite part of the story.
> Point to your favorite character. Draw his or her picture.
> Point to what the character does that you like.
> Is this character _____ or _____? (Provide either/or questions that embed the answer in the question.)
> (Show a range of familiar book covers.) Which story is this one most like?

Journaling. There are a variety of ways in which journals are designed to foster reflection about the reading experience. To facilitate imagining, use illustrative journals that involve verbal and pictorial reflection. The unique feature of illustrative journals is the combination of verbal and nonverbal reflection. Each page is a landscape layout with three components. The first is a column for drawing a picture, the second is space for page citations and a name or subtitle of the drawing, and the third is a column for reflective writing about the picture.

Illustrative Journal Page Layout

Draw a picture from the story	*Write about the picture*

Citation (page and name): _____

Tip for parent involvement: Use the above journal format as an illustrated home reading log.

Guided imagery. This technique can be used to help students expand imaginative experience with a story. A significant function of guided imagery is to help students place themselves in the story. Conducting guided imagery is relatively simple. All it requires is a picture from the story that students can see. The picture may come from an illustration in the book, from a teacher-made sketch, or a student drawing. If you create a sketch or ask a student to make a drawing, be sure that it is large enough for the class to see clearly from their seats.

Following is a set of sample directions for guided imagery. In this sample, the guide asks the students to place themselves in the picture of a scene from Beatrix Potter's *The Tale of Peter Rabbit*. Each direction calls the students to an ever closer place in the story picture. You will need to adapt the directions to fit the picture that you select for this activity.

Guided Imagery Sample Directions

1. Look at a picture of this tree. Peter Rabbit lives at the base of this tree.

2. Look at the grass surrounding the tree with Mr. MacGregor's garden in the background.

3. Do you see the road winding by the tree? Picture yourself walking on the road.

4. How do you feel? Warm? Cold? Dry? Wet? Is the wind blowing?

5. Walk up to the tree and look beyond it. Do you see Mr. MacGregor in his garden? What is he doing?

6. Hide behind the tree. Here comes a rabbit. What is it doing?

7. Follow the rabbit through the door at the base of the tree. Can you fit? Squeeze in.

8. How does it look inside the tree? Dark? Light? Are there windows?

9. How big is the inside? As you look around, what do you see?

10. Can you feel the fur of other rabbits? What does it smell like?

11. Peter's mother is serving food and something to drink. What is it? How does it taste?

12. In your illustrative journals, draw a picture of Peter's home and write about your visit there.

TABLE 6.5   *Visualizing and Imagining*

	Beginning	Early Intermediate and Intermediate	Early Advanced and Advanced
Visualizing	• Work with a more advanced partner to create pictures from story scenes • Collaborate to arrange pictures on a story ladder with assistance	• Identify initial events, connected actions, climax, and resulting events in a story • Draw and arrange pictures on a story ladder.	(Same as prior level) • Differentiate between climax and denouement
Imagining	• Draw a favorite part of the story in a journal • Label significant features and/or events • Draw a picture of yourself in the story	• Maintain an illustrative journal with citations, reflections, and pictures • Write responses to aesthetic questions in a journal • Draw yourself into the story in a variety of places and perspectives	(Same as prior level) • Discuss and/or write about placing yourself in the story from a variety of places in the setting

Shared Read-Aloud Activities

Shared read-aloud activities can take a variety of forms depending on the teacher's purpose for the activity. By grouping students strategically, teachers address social and instructional needs and avoid placing ELLs at risk of embarrassment by reading aloud to others. Strategic grouping requires knowing the proficiency levels of the students as well as other needs. In order to address social-interactive aspects of reading, group students according to similar reading levels so that they read and discuss the story within a comfort-level group. The purpose of mixed levels is to help address the needs of less proficient readers by partnering them with more proficient reading models.

Tip for parent involvement: Give children an assignment to read a short book or a selected passage to as many members of the family as possible. This shares the reading experience, motivates the child, and develops reading fluency.

Identifying the reading level of students requires an assessment tool. There are a number of tools available such as running records (Clay, 1997). For rapid assessment purposes, I recommend a read-aloud rubric. Table 6.6 is a rubric for evaluating how a student reads aloud according to all five levels of proficiency. The rubric evaluates three areas of reading aloud: fluency, expression, and comprehension and critique. Fluency refers to the pacing the student uses while reading. Expression refers to the appropriate use of intonation while reading aloud. Finally, it is possible to memorize a passage and repeat it aloud with fluency and expression without comprehension;

however, that would not be reading. Reading by its very definition is a process of making meaning of text (Smith, 1985). Therefore, the rubric includes a component for evaluating comprehension.

Fluency, as described in the rubric, is composed of multiple skills. In this simple rubric three areas make up an evaluation of fluency. Pace, or fluidity, is the first component. The next component is the amount of text, whether it be selected words, sentences, paragraphs, or lengthy selections. Finally, recognition of errors and self-correction are important aspects of fluency. Keep in mind that as the student advances the number of errors decreases; self-correction decreases with increased levels of fluency as well.

Expression, as described in the rubric, is appropriate intonation while reading aloud. This involves changes of intonation as called for by the text. Initially, a reader may sound monotone, or even "robotic," while reading word for word. As proficiency develops, the reader recognizes indicators of change in expression, such as ending punctuation. Advanced readers interpret the mood of text and enhance the reading with a wide range of expression.

Comprehension is a much more involved skill than described in this rubric. The reason for a simple rendering of comprehension here is to make it useful for the rubric assessment. It is my opinion that an overly complex assessment tool will not be useful for rapid assessment. The essential components of comprehension for the purposes of the rubric begin with recognition of story events and characters. It builds on events and characters in terms of increasing depth of understanding of how events and characters relate to the overall plot and other stories. The other area is the development of a personal critique of the story. Advanced readers readily establish a justified critique of the text.

Using the rubric is quite simple. Begin with a reading selection that includes characters and story events. Be sure to select a passage that the student has not read before to ensure the validity of the evaluation. Ask the student to read aloud. Note indicators for levels of fluency and expression in the rubric and match the student's reading to the appropriate level. (A good rule of thumb

TABLE 6.6   *Rubric for Reading Aloud*

	Beginning	Early Intermediate	Intermediate	Early Advanced	Advanced
Fluency	• Silent • May recognize some words	• Reads word for word with frequent pauses at unknown words • Reads simple sentences • Little error recognition • Occasional self-correction	• Reads separate sentences fluently (may pause between sentences) • Reads more complex sentences and paragraphs • Recognizes errors and self-corrects	• Fluid, with some errors • Reads multiple paragraphs with relative ease • Rapid self-correction	• Exceptionally fluid with few to no errors • Reads lengthy passages with ease • Little to no need for self-correction
Expression	• No expression in reading	• Little to no change in intonation • May sound monotone or "robotic"	• Changes intonation at exclamation points or question marks	• Reads to an audience • Changes intonation in appropriate places	• Interprets the mood of the text by reading with a range of expression

Comprehension and Critique	• Little to no comprehension	• Identifies story events • Recognizes characters	• Identifies and describes story events • Identifies and describes character traits	• Identifies and describes how story events relate to the overall plot • Compares and contrasts character roles • Establishes an initial critique	• Discusses plot as it relates to previous reading • Describes the author's perspective of characters • Readily provides justification for a critique

with rubric evaluation is that when a borderline evaluation occurs, assess the student at the lower level. This is not intended to stigmatize a student, but rather trigger additional assistance. In other words, in order to attain a specific level, the student must clearly demonstrate that level of ability. It does ELLs no favors to be assessed above their ability level.) At the end of the reading, ask the following questions to assess comprehension, and compare the student responses against the criteria for comprehension and critique:

> Can you tell me about the story you just read?
> What can you tell me about the characters?
> (Continue with the following if the student demonstrates considerable comprehension):
> Did you enjoy the story? Why?

Same-level groupings. Once the students are assessed according to reading levels, the teacher can make choices about shared reading activities. Same-level students can simply take turns reading selections together as pairs. Less proficient readers would read shorter passages of one sentence to a single paragraph at a time. With more proficient readers, increase the length of the selection from one to more paragraphs. In small group settings, students can read a selection and then call on another student to continue reading. Consider a random reading activity in which students read favorite selections without regard to the order.

Random Reading Activity (for same-level groupings)

1. Prior to reading, set the parameters of the reading selection (give page numbers or a selection of paragraphs that maintain a theme).

2. Allow a few minutes for students to review the reading.

3. Ask students to choose a favorite passage to share.

4. Ask students to read their favorite passage to a partner as a rehearsal. (Encourage students to help each other pronounce words or to ask for help with difficult words.)

5. Open up the entire group to read their selected passages in the order of their choosing.

6. Ask students, Why was that selection important to you?

7. Ask students to highlight and summarize the important points of the reading selections.

8. Record the summary statements on chart paper so that all can see.

9. Invite students to write about their understanding of the reading in their journals.

Mixed-level groupings. This type of grouping addresses the needs of a less proficient reader by providing a model. The more proficient reader is placed in the role of exemplary reader, which increases their level of attention to the reading task. Reading formats may be either leapfrog reading or model and repeat reading. Leapfrog reading is just as it sounds: The exemplary reader reads one selection and the less proficient reader reads the following selection. The exemplary reader is called on to monitor and to demonstrate how to read difficult words or sentences.

Model and repeat reading is most appropriate when the less proficient reader is a struggling reader. Model and repeat begins with the exemplary reader reading a sentence or paragraph. Then the less proficient reader reads the same passage. If the less proficient reader struggles, they both read the passage again. Avoid rereading too much, which may lead to discouraging both readers. Limit to two rereads and then move on.

Leapfrog and model and repeat strategies are not limited to a single classroom setting. These are also appropriate strategies for cross-age tutoring. Establish a partnership with a classroom at another grade level.

Rules for Leapfrog Reading	*Rules for Model and Repeat Reading*
1. Take turns reading.	1. Teacher assigns partner #1 and partner #2.
2. Listen while your partner is reading.	2. Partner #1 reads first.
3. Always be courteous.	3. Partner #2 follows by reading the same words.
4. What to say to help correct an error:	4. Listen while your partner is reading.
"I read the word like this . . ."	5. Read the same section again if needed.
"Listen to me read the word."	6. Always be courteous.
"Let's read this sentence together."	7. What to say to help correct an error:
"Good job!" "That's right!" "Nice reading."	"I read the word like this . . ."
	"Listen as I read the word."
	"Let's read this sentence together."
	"Good job!" "That's right!" "Nice reading."

Developing a Love for the Task

A key to reading instruction is to develop a love for the task. Returning to the running analogy, the pleasurable feeling a runner experiences from the release of endorphins is called a "runner's high." The same can be true about reading. Developing a love for the task is a "reader's high." There are a number of ways to develop a love for the task. Reading to children with feeling and enthusiasm, giving ample opportunities to read, and providing students with a wide selection of books are significant ways to foster a love of reading. Discussed below are three strategies that contribute to developing a love for the task of reading. First, using a reading interest inventory helps match books to a student's area of interest. Second, utilizing criteria for quality literature helps in selecting wonderful books. Third, teaching the student an easy strategy to avoid choosing a book that is in the frustration level fosters independence in the selection process.

Reading interest inventory. The following is a suggested reading interest inventory. Less proficient ELLs would need assistance in filling it out. More proficient students would be able to complete it in a short period of time.

Reading Interest Inventory

Name _____   Date: _____

1. List your favorite stories or book titles:
    *
    *
    *

2. List your favorite story characters:
    *
    *
    *

3. Which do you prefer? _____ Fiction _____ Nonfiction

4. Check which genres you have read and circle the ones you like best:

    _____ Fantasy   _____ Mythology   _____ Adventure   _____ Historical Fiction

    _____ Mystery   _____ Horror Stories   _____ Poetry   _____ Comedy

    _____ Biography   _____ Historical   _____ Scientific   _____ Pop Culture

    _____ OTHER_____

5. Check which topics interest you:

    _____ Exotic Places   _____ Animals   _____ People   _____ Technology   _____ Jokes

    _____ Outer Space   _____ Nature   _____ Cars/Motorcycles _____ Sports   _____ Music

    _____ Outdoor Adventure   _____ Fashion   _____ Monsters   _____ Magic   _____ Movies

    _____ Presidents/Leaders _____ OTHER _____

6. What are you reading at this time?_____

    Did you select it? _____ Yes _____ No

    If so, why? _____

    What is your opinion about it? _____

Rating quality books. The process of selecting quality books requires both a rating instrument and selection criteria. Below is a four-point rating instrument for quality children's books. The reason for a four-point system is to force a decision of whether the book meets criteria or is below criteria. Consider using this rating system for yourself, as teacher, or as an activity for students to do individually or in a group.

The selection criteria listed in the rating instrument address six areas of quality literature: vivid illustrations, character development, engaging story, cultural perspective or diversity, English language development possibilities, and connections to other curricular areas.

Vivid illustrations are essential for ELLs because they contribute to comprehension of the story. Meaningful illustrations provide context and understanding of story events, and also enhance the beauty of the reading experience.

Character development and an engaging story are quality criteria for anyone choosing a book to read. The richness of a good story is dependent on character development and the story's level of engagement. One consideration is that as students mature and change, their notion of an engaging story develops as well.

The cultural perspective or diversity criterion requires some explanation. Identifying a story's cultural perspective—for example, Latino, Anglo, Asian, African American, Persian, Indian, and so forth—is not necessarily to match a story to one's cultural background, but to identify, appreciate, and share cultural insights in our literary world. A distinct cultural perspective provides a reference point for talking about the similarities and differences of one's own culture. Diversity refers to multiple cultural perspectives portrayed in the story as opposed to a single cultural portrayal.

Considering English language development possibilities simply means asking the following question: What can this book teach about English? One book might utilize expansive verbs to show action, another might employ rich descriptive words, and another might use similes for metaphorical thinking. Great books use a wide range of linguistic devices.

Connections to other curricular areas means identifying how a book can contribute to a thematic unit of study. Begin by looking at the setting of story. Is it in a place or time period that is going to be studied in a geography or history lesson? Does the book deal with social science issues? Look for visual and performing arts connections to dance, music, theater, or visual arts.

Using the rating instrument is a matter of reading or previewing a story with the criteria in mind. Place a check in each row under the appropriate number rating. Subtotal and then total the points. Divide the total by six for an average score. Include reviewer comments to highlight unique aspects of a book.

Rating Instrument for Quality Books:
4 = Exceeds criteria, 3 = Meets criteria, 2 = Below criteria, 1 = Unacceptable or N/A

Selection Criteria	*4*	*3*	*2*	*1*
Vivid illustrations				
Character development				
Engaging story				
Cultural perspective or diversity				
English language development possibilities				
Connections to other curricular areas. Note curricular area(s):				
Subtotal				
Total	÷ by 6 = Average _____			

Reviewer's comments:

The five-finger test for self-selected reading. Helping students select books within their reading level is as easy as counting to five. Ask students to select a book and begin to read the first page or a random passage. As they read, tell them to hold up a closed fist lightly and in a comfortable position. Each time the students come across a word they can't read, they hold up a finger. If they get to five fingers before they finish a paragraph, the book is probably at a frustration level. Students who read without raising a finger will either have a readable book, or one that is too easy for their level.

The five-finger test is not a hard and fast rule, nor is it without its exceptions. Sometimes a wonderful book will require work on the part of the reader. There is no harm in encouraging a student to tackle a challenging book. Conversely, we do not want to encourage selecting a book solely because it is an easy read. The five-finger test is limited in its use, but it does give a motivated reader a quick way to assess the level of difficulty the book will pose.

Recording Progress

Reading logs. A runner in training logs mileage and a training regime. Readers can track their progress and log reading experiences as well. There are a number of ways to log reading in order to track student progress. The three formats discussed here—training logs, home reading logs, and conversational book reports—are for classroom and/or home use. Using all three might prove to be too much; treat them as a list of suggested tools to choose from.

Training logs. Training logs are student-managed logs for classroom reading. A page of a training log will cover a five-day period. Students will record the date, title, author and genre, reading type, page numbers, and the number of minutes each day. At the end of a five-day period the student can total the number of pages and minutes. There is also a comments section for each day where the student can make a notation about the reading experience. Comments may include a highlight in the story, a difficulty, new vocabulary, or a literary response to the reading. The reading type refers to the kind of reading the student is attempting such as an easy read, a tempo read, or a long read.

A reader's training log has several functions. It is used to record reading information. When multiple pages are logged in, the student can compare the number of pages and time spent reading from week to week. This can also be used to develop and monitor reading goals for number of pages and minutes spent reading.

Another function of the log is for planning a reading schedule. The student can fill in several of the columns ahead of time such as title and author, reading type, and minutes. When the day comes, the student can record the date, the number of pages read, and any comments. Planning ahead by using the log can save time in classroom transitions. If a student has the log programmed for a week, little to no time will be spent by the teacher telling the student what to read.

Reader's Training Log

Date	Title/Author/Genre	Reading Type	Number of Pages	Number of Minutes
Comments:				
Comments:				
Comments:				
Comments:				
Comments:				
Total of pages and minutes				

Home reading logs. These are similar to training logs with a few differences. A home reading log is used for a month at a time and is maintained by the student and family members. It requires a signature from a parent or guardian for verification purposes. It also has a section at the bottom for recording total pages and minutes read. Consider maintaining a graph of each student's pages and minutes read at home each week. This will be important data for reporting to parents and school staff. It can also be used as a friendly competition in the classroom to acknowledge and reward persistent reading at home.

Home Reading Log

Date	Title/Author/Genre	Number of Pages	Number of Minutes	Signature
Total		**pages**	**minutes**	

Tip for parent involvement: Initially, maintain home reading logs on a weekly basis. The students turn in their logs each Friday for teacher review and credit. On Mondays send out a new page. Once the rhythm is established, move to a bi-weekly schedule and then a monthly schedule.

Conversational book reports. This activity involves classroom volunteers who assist in the reading progress of each student. Each time a student completes a story or book, he signs up to report to a classroom volunteer. The classroom volunteer takes a three-by-five index card and records the student's name, the date, book title, author, and genre, and then asks the student, "Tell me about the book." The student, in turn, talks about the book, and the volunteer records a summary of what the student says.

The purpose of this report is twofold. First, it gives the student the opportunity to talk about a book with an interested party. The interactive nature of a conversational report is highly motivating for readers. One of the great pleasures of reading is to talk to someone else about the story.

The second purpose is to record the number of books read by individual students and to obtain an aggregate number of books being read by an entire class. The cards can either be filed in a student portfolio or be displayed on a bulletin board showing the total number of books read to date.

Conversational Book Report

Student Name _____ Date _____

Book Title _____

Author _____ Genre _____

Oral Report _____

_____

_____

_____

Recorder's Name: _____

Tip for parent involvement: Parents can involve extended family members in taking conversational book reports. Often an older sibling will do the writing on behalf of a parent who is not literate in English.

Charting classroom reading. Charting classroom reading takes two basic forms: displays and teacher records. Displays can be in the form of a bulletin board class record, a chart in graph form, and/or creative display such as a bookworm.

Displays. A bulletin board display that I recommend is to show the number of books the class has read by mounting the Conversational Book Report index cards. Divide up the bulletin board into a grid using yarn. Staple the yarn to the bulletin board at intersecting points. Map out the grid so that the name of each student in the classroom is mounted in a square in the grid. Also in each grid square, mount a clip to hold the index cards for each book the student has read. To one side of the bulletin board, mount a large paper cutout of a thermometer with markings for every 100 books read. In the round base of the thermometer, glue a card that records the total number of books read in class. Give the bulletin board a title, such as "Look How Many Books We've Read" or "Can We Read 1,000 Books?" Each time a student completes a Conversational Book Report card, it is clipped next to her name. Each month, students total their cards and a small group of students update the bulletin board and color in the thermometer with the appropriate number of books read to date.

Class reading graphs are a way to show quantitative data about student reading. As mentioned above in "Repetitive reading for time," use the table that records the change in time from the first reading to the second. A longer interval can be recorded so that it displays the difference from one month to the next in number of words read per minute.

Other displays include linear graphs of total number of pages and/or total minutes read each week based upon the data collected from the home reading log or the student training log. They can be recorded by individual or group pages. Consider grouping students into teams and recording total pages read each week in a friendly competition.

Creative classroom displays, like a giant bookworm, is another way to show classroom reading. A giant bookworm is a series of green circles (painted paper plates or colored paper) aligned in a linear fashion with each circle overlapping to give the appearance of the worm's body. The head has a face, but each circle in the body of the worm is a book title. With every book a student reads, a new circle is added to lengthen the body and the worm grows. To increase motivation, the student who read the book has his name displayed on the bookworm by the title.

Teacher records. Record keeping is an essential part of charting student progress. Using the read-aloud rubric to assess reading levels, the teacher can record a student's level on a trimester basis. At three points during the year, the teacher can listen to a student read and record the level of proficiency using a class record (see sample). The notion is as follows: B = beginning, EI = early intermediate, I = intermediate, EA = early advanced, and A = advanced. Once a student is assessed, the teacher need only record the name of the student and circle the appropriate letter.

Class Record of Level of Proficiency

Student	1st Trimester			2nd Trimester			3rd Trimester		
	B	EI-I	EA-A	B	EI-I	EA-A	B	EI-I	EA-A
	B	EI-I	EA-A	B	EI-I	EA-A	B	EI-I	EA-A
	B	EI-I	EA-A	B	EI-I	EA-A	B	EI-I	EA-A
	B	EI-I	EA-A	B	EI-I	EA-A	B	EI-I	EA-A
	B	EI-I	EA-A	B	EI-I	EA-A	B	EI-I	EA-A
	B	EI-I	EA-A	B	EI-I	EA-A	B	EI-I	EA-A

Another form of record keeping is compiling data from the home reading log. Each month, students turn in a home reading log with total minutes and pages read, and the teacher records the numbers that have been verified in the home log on a class monthly record of reading.

Class Monthly Record of Reading in Total Minutes and Pages

Student	Sept	Oct	Nov	Dec	Jan	Feb	Mar	Apr	May	Jun
mins										
pgs										
mins										
pgs										
mins										
pgs										

Appendix: Getting Started with PowerPoint

Creating a New Presentation

1. Open PowerPoint
2. Dialog Box "Create a new presentation"
   –select a design template
   –select a background
   (Navigate with < > arrow keys on the keyboard)
3. Select a title slide from the slide auto layout dialog box.

Text

Adding Text

1. Click in the "click to add title" text box
2. Repeat for the subtitle (Keep statements brief)

Repositioning Text Boxes "Click & Drag"

1. Click inside a text box. When the crossed-arrow cursor appears, hold down the mouse button and drag the text box to the new location.
2. Resize the text box by positioning the cursor on a corner. When the arrow cursor appears, click and drag to size the text box.

Modifying Text

1. Click and drag the cursor over a line of text to select or highlight.
2. Use the toolbar (top of screen) to change font, color, size of text.

Adding Slides

1. Click on new slide icon on the toolbar or "Insert."
2. Select auto layout from the "New Slide" screen. Click OK.

Moving Between Slides

1. Click on the "Slide Sorter View" on the toolbar in the bottom left corner.
2. Select a slide.
3. Repeat #1.

Changing Slide Order

1. Click on the "Slide Sorter View" on the toolbar in the bottom left corner.
2. Move a slide to a different order:
   –Click and drag the selected slide to the desired position
   –Lift the mouse button when in position
3. Exit "Slide Sorter View" by double-clicking on one of the slides.

Adding Clipart

1. Using a slide layout with a "Clipart" box, double click on the "Clipart" icon.
2. Or, add clipart: click on "Insert" on the toolbar, "Picture" and "Clipart."
3. The Clipart Gallery displays a library of pictures for selection.

4. External clipart can be copied and pasted by selecting the picture with a right mouse click on PCs or holding down the mouse button on Macs.
5. Paste the picture on the slide: Hold down the control key and press the "V" key.
6. Reposition clipart using "click & drag" when the crossed-arrow cursor appears.
7. Resize clipart using "click & drag" when the arrow cursor appears on the edge of the picture.

Adding Transitions

Multiple Slide Transitions

1. Click on the "Slide Sorter View" on the toolbar in the bottom left corner.
2. Click "Edit" and "Select All" from the upper toolbar menu.
3. Click on the "Transition" icon, far left just under the toolbar.
4. Under "Effect," select the transition(s) you want.
5. Select "Apply to All."
6. View the transitions: Click on "Slide Show View" on the toolbar.
7. Click on the first slide of the presentation.

Single Slide Transition and/or Sounds

1. Click on the "Slide Sorter View" on the toolbar in the bottom left corner.
2. Select the slide you want to create a transition from.
3. Click "Tools," "Slide Transition."
4. Select "Effect," choose a desired effect.
5. Choose whether to activate the transition by mouse click under "Advance."
6. Add sound to the transition by selecting a desired sound from the "Sound Menu." Select "Okay."

Adding Animations

1. Click "Slide Show," "Custom Animation."
2. Click on each graphic or text object you want to animate in the upper left-hand corner of the dialog box.
3. Click and drag to select the "Effect" you desire.
4. Order the appearance of the animations: click on the object and then on the green arrow below.
5. Under "Start Animation," leave it on Mouse Click.
6. Preview the animation by clicking on the preview animation button.

References

Clay, M. M. (1997). *Running records for classroom teachers.* Portsmouth, NH: Heinemann.

Cox, C. (2004). *Teaching Language Arts: A child-centered and response-centered approach.* Boston, MA: Allyn & Bacon.

Garcia, G. (2000). Bilingual children's reading. In M. L. Kamil, P. B. Mosenthal, P. D. Pearson, & R. Barr (Eds.), *Handbook of reading research,* Vol. III (pp. 813–834). Mahwah, NJ: Earlbaum.

Gordon, C. J. & Braun, C. (1983). Using story schema as an aid to reading and writing. *The Reading Teacher, 37*(2), 116–121.

Reese, L., Garnier, H., Gallimore, R., & Goldenberg, C. (2000). Longitudinal analysis of the antecedents of emergent Spanish literacy and middle-school English reading achievement of Spanish-speaking students. *American Educational Research Journal, 37*(3), 633–662.

Reutzel, D. R., & Cooter, R. B. (2004). *Teaching children to read: Putting the pieces together.* (4th ed.). Columbus, OH: Pearson/Merrill-Prentice Hall.

Rosenblatt, L. (1978). *The reader, the text, the poem.* Carbondale, IL: Southern Illinois University Press.

Slavin, R., & Cheung, A. (2003). *Effective reading programs for English language learners: A best-evidence synthesis.* Report No. 66. Center for Research on the Education of Students Placed at Risk (CRESPAR), Grant No. R117-D40005 from the Institute of Education Sciences. Baltimore, MD: Johns Hopkins University.

Sadoski, M., & Quast, Z. (1990). Reader response and long-term recall for journalistic text: The roles of imagery, affect and importance. *Reading Research Quarterly, 24*(4), 256–272.

Smith, F. (1988). *Understanding reading.* (4th ed.). Hillsdale, NJ: Erlbaum.

7

Teaching Writing Across Proficiency Levels

TESOL Goals and Standards

   GOAL 3: *To use English in socially and culturally appropriate ways*

   Standard 1: *Students will use the appropriate language variety, register, and genre according to audience, purpose, and setting*

   Standard 2: *Students will use nonverbal communication appropriate to audience, purpose, and setting*

   Standard 3: *Students will use appropriate learning strategies to extend their sociolinguistic and sociocultural competence*

All Children are Writers

Simply put, novice writers must write in order to learn to write well. There is no other way. Sit down at a desk. Scratch out ideas individually or as a group. Write for an authentic purpose. Remember that ideas come first and that conventions follow. Don't be afraid to make mistakes; errors are easy to fix. Discuss the writing with other writers. Craft the writing with revisions and editing. Find an outlet to show the work, to make it public, to publish. But the fundamental assumption is that all children are writers.

All children can write. Given the opportunity, they express themselves in written form. The teacher's task, therefore, is to take the unconventional, raw writing and guide the child to craft it into a conventional form.

The purpose of this chapter is to present strategies for teaching the writing process (Graves, 1984) across levels of English language proficiency. The strategies are adapted according to beginning, intermediate, and advanced levels of proficiency. This does not mean that there is no difference between students on an early intermediate and intermediate level or an early advanced and advanced level. It simply means that many of the writing strategies suggested below address multiple levels of proficiency. Often the accommodations for early intermediate or early advanced students are made in terms of the length or complexity of the written product rather than the strategy used for teaching the writing process.

The writing process provides one way to organize strategies for English Language Learners. Graves's (1994) organization outlines prewriting, drafting, revision, editing, and publication. Another way to approach writing is in terms of collaborative, interactive, and individual writing activities. These kinds of activities map onto the writing process and provide strategic ways to help ELLs across levels of proficiency. Collaboration helps the beginning writer to develop entry-level skills in the writing process. Collaboration also creates a social-interactive forum for writing as a team for a singular purpose. Collaborative activities include chart stories, collaborative story interviews, semantic mapping, paragraph coding and outlining, making big books, developing class newsletters, and even composing songs and poems.

Interactive writing is a shared experience like a dialog on paper. Interactive strategies mediate development in writing. Some of the strategies include interactive journals, lap board modeling, and rubric partnering in which a more experienced writer interacts with the novice writer. Vygotsky's (1978) notion of a zone of proximal development is realized in a one-to-one relationship in this kind of interactive arrangement.

Individualized strategies include many of the aforementioned collaborative and interactive strategies done on an individual basis plus dual-entry journal writing, composing poetry, reporting narrative or informational prose, and making personal books. There is overlap to be sure, but collaborative, interactive, and individual strategies can cover multiple skills across all levels of proficiency.

Although writing is referred to as a process, we assess writing as a product in a variety of ways. Assessment of writing can be designed to match the product whether it be collaborative, individual, or across proficiency levels. In this chapter, I will provide several ways to assess writing including a rubric builder for tailoring assessment to a specific writing assignment.

Tip for parent involvement: Encourage parents to maintain a writing center at home. A writing center can be as simple as a box of writing materials (pencils, erasers, paper, pencil sharpener, dictionary, thesaurus, and a writing tablet). Having a designated place for writing with sufficient materials can greatly enhance the home–school connection.

The Writing Process

The writing process outlines a sequence, or stages, that writers work through. Teaching process writing provides students with essential guidance and tools to craft their writing. It helps establish goals for each writing project. The process appears to be a fixed set of stages, but in reality there is an organic and recursive quality to it. Writers move back and forth between drafting, revising, and editing. Certain revisions may require further prewriting. Also, a change in publishing formats may trigger additional revisions. The writing process, in other words, is deeper and more complex than any single framework can describe.

Prewrite	Draft	Revise	Edit	Publish
• Draw on experiences • Read/listen to stories • Generate ideas • Organize thinking • Talk over ideas	• Put ideas on paper • Focus on meaning over conventions • Experiment	• Reread during/after writing draft • Rethink what is written	• Proofread revised piece • Talk to teacher in editing conference	• Choose the form: -book -display in room -drama -reader's theater

• Choose type of writing: journals, letters, expressive writing, articles, literature model • Consider audience • Brainstorm ideas: list, cluster, quick write • Rehearse: draw, talk, map, plot, diagram, act out	• Understand that writing will change • Try out different possibilities • Talk over drafts with others • Rehearse some more	• Share with others in a reader's circle • Talk to the teacher in a writer's conference • Change, add to, delete, modify, rearrange paragraphs • Expand ideas	• Ask for help in peer-editing conference • Rephrase and refine (select a more descriptive word) • Check: spelling, punctuation, capitalization, usage, form, legibility • Identify errors and correct own work	-electronic media -letter -big book -newspaper article -poster -advertisement • Share published pieces: -read aloud to the class -reader's circle -author's chair -writer's workshop

(Graves, 1984)

Prewriting is like preparing the soil before planting a seed. It involves exploring the source of writing such as one's own experiences or events in history, reading resources and listening to stories, researching information, and/or sharing ideas. Ideas tend to germinate and sprout in random ways, so they need an organizer that can be used to quickly get them on paper. Various prewriting organizers will be discussed below in the context of specific activities.

Drafting is the raw, initial writing. The primary focus is getting ideas on paper, with conventions as a secondary focus. This is not to say that conventions are unimportant; it is only to emphasize what comes first. Based on my personal teaching experience, if a child is a frustrated writer, it is often related to a struggle with conventions before developing ideas. The novice writer may need particular help with scripting ideas to be able to continue in the writing process. Once the ideas are germinated and drafted, the conventions can be dealt with in the revisions and editing phases. In other words, develop the notion of drafting ideas with the understanding that the initial draft will change.

(*A note about the use of computers in the classroom.* Encourage students to draft their writing at the computer using a word-processing program. Print out the drafts for revision and editing as a hard copy. Then return to the computer for inputting changes. Many teachers hold off on using computers until the final drafts, but writing initial drafts at the computer will make the other phases of the writing process go so much easier, for example, by moving paragraphs with cut-and-paste features, correcting spelling using a spell-checker, and changing formats, font styles, and layouts. Beginning with word processing from the outset gives the student a wide range of media formats to choose from for publishing at the end of the writing process, as well.)

Revision is the place where the writer takes the audience into account. How to make the writing clearer is of primary concern. The simplest way to initiate revision is to have students read their writing aloud to each other. When students read aloud their writing, they begin to note missing or out-of-order parts, to hear mistakes, and to identify unclear wording that they may have missed while writing. They begin to see flaws because, as they read aloud, they become the audience of their own writing. Reading to a partner provides additional input especially when students are apprised of rubric criteria for the writing ahead of time.

Editing is the easiest phase of the writing process to teach explicitly. It takes a careful reader to edit for grammar, punctuation, spelling, and style; but these corrections can be marked directly on a hard copy. Students participating in a rhythm of writing in a classroom setting learn to expect to get editorial markings on their papers. Editing can be time consuming; however, if

TABLE 7.1 *Writing Activities across Levels of Proficiency*

Writing Activities	*Beginning*	*Early Intermediate and Intermediate*	*Early Advanced and Advanced*
Collaborative	• Collaborative story interviews • Graphic organizers—cluster map, tree map • Making big books • Triante poetry frames	(Same as prior level) • Song/poetry word banks and frames • Correspondence centers	(Same as prior level) • Team writing projects • Organizing multiple sections of larger project writing • Edited collections, newsletters, project reports
Interactive	• Interactive journals • Lap board modeling	• Family journals • Pen pals	(Same as prior level) • Web-based discussion boards, or newsgroups
Individual	• Pictorial journals • Making personal illustrated books	(Same as prior level) • Double-entry journals • Informational report frames	(Same as prior level) • Persuasive writing

students are included in the editing process many of the errors can be addressed prior to the teacher having to review the writing. The students' unedited writing also becomes the source for various mini-lessons that the teacher may give at the beginning of a writing workshop time.

Publishing writing is preparing a work to show in public. There are numerous venues and various media available to teachers to display a student's writing.

The writing process is often viewed as linear. Theoretically, the writer moves lock-step from one stage to the next. The reality, however, is that the type of writing activity one selects dictates the stages of the process. Depending on the intentions of the writer, certain forms of journaling, for example, may not necessarily employ extensive prewriting or revision. The writer's purpose may be more of a free-flowing, "stream of consciousness" style of writing with no intention of it being displayed for publication. Other writing activities such as collaborative story interviewing combine prewriting and drafting simultaneously.

In Table 7.1, various writing activities are organized according to collaborative, interactive, and individual writing. Most of the activities map onto all of the stages of the writing process. They are described according to the sequence of appropriate stages of the writing process.

Beginning Level

Collaborative Writing Activities for Beginning Level

Collaborative story interview. This is an activity that is appropriate for beginning-level students, but is easily adapted for all levels. (Adaptations are inserted in parentheses.) In short, a collaborative story interview activity is a group interview of one person. The students ask questions and then tell the teacher what to write on a chart. The teacher facilitates the process by acting as the "scribe" for beginning-level students. This activity also features a coding technique to identify like sentences and order them into paragraphs.

Preparation

1. Materials: Two sheets of lined chart paper, four different colored marking pens, student paper, pencils, and crayons or colored pencils.

2. Choose a student to be interviewed by the class. This may be a star of the week, a random selection, a child playing the role of a story character, or a special guest such as an adult visiting the class.

3. The interviewee chooses who will ask each question. If the interviewee does not wish to respond, she simply says, "pass." An optional rule is that the interviewee alternates fielding questions from boys and girls to ensure gender equity in the process.

Prewriting and Drafting

1. The teacher stands to one side ready to write the students' responses on a large sheet of chart paper. (Early intermediate and intermediate students should be given paper and pencils to write what the teacher models on the chart. Early advanced and advanced students are encouraged to formulate their own sentences.)

2. An important strategy: Instead of writing the students' responses verbatim, the teacher asks the student who posed the question to paraphrase in his own words what the response was. Example:

Interviewer: Where were you born?
Interviewee: In Jalisco, Mexico.
Teacher (asking the interviewer): What do I write?
Interviewer: She was born in Jalisco, Mexico.

3. There are several reasons for having the student paraphrase the responses: (A) Paraphrasing changes the answer from first to third person. This produces a narrative style. (B) Asking students to paraphrase what their fellow students have said teaches them to be active listeners. (C) If an interviewer struggles with how to paraphrase a response, the class becomes involved in negotiating an accurate representation of the response.

4. The teacher writes the paraphrased sentence on the chart paper and the students copy the sentence on their own sheet of paper. (Early intermediate and intermediate students can write the sentence on the chart. To guide the writing, the teacher uses a small white board and dry erase marker to help spell words. If a student makes an error on the chart, cover the mistake with a small piece of white correction tape and write the correction on top of it.)

5. While writing, the teacher uses the student's language to teach punctuation, spelling, and grammatical issues. Features of the writing are highlighted with a different color pen and discussed with the entire class.

Revision

1. At the end of the interview the sentences written on the chart are in random order, so the next step is to group like sentences and order them.

2. Code similar sentences with a symbol, such as a red triangle for sentences concerning family, a blue square for sentences concerning dreams and aspirations, and a green circle for sentences concerning school. Students will color code sentences on their papers.

3. Decide which group should be first in the sequence and number the sentences in order of preference within each coded group. In this way, students begin to see the formation of paragraphs around an idea or theme.

4. Rewrite the interview responses in paragraph form according to the coded and numbered sequence. The teacher rewrites the chart story, and the students rewrite their individual copies as a homework assignment.

Editing

1. When the homework draft is returned, the teacher will ask the students to review a partner's copy for grammar, spelling, and punctuation. Beginning through intermediate students compare their partner's work against the story chart prepared by the teacher. Early advanced through advanced students check work and provide comments.

2. Students rewrite the edited draft for homework.

Publication

1. The large chart story is illustrated by selected students.

2. The finished chart story can be displayed on a bulletin board. Another option is to bind the chart story with other pages to form a collaborative class big book.

Prewriting with graphic organizers for beginners. Graphic organizers are used predominantly in the prewriting stage of the writing process, although they are sometimes displayed within the body of a larger piece to illustrate the relationships between ideas. Organizing writing graphically works to give an overview of the entire piece at a glance. There are any number of ways to organize writing graphically, but two organizers in particular are helpful for process writing with beginners: a cluster map and a tree map. Cluster maps and tree maps work together. The cluster map helps record ideas in random order, while the tree map is used to arrange the clustered ideas in organized categories. Each organizer has its function and adaptations for proficiency levels.

Cluster maps. Also called semantic maps or circle maps, cluster maps are designed to record initial ideas in a random order. Begin with a central idea written or illustrated at the center of a piece of paper. For example, a picture of the main character of the story could occupy the center of the map. The teacher writes the students' words around the center as they identify and describe the main character. Some cluster maps are drawn as two concentric circles. One small circle in the middle contains the central idea, and another large circle functions as a border for the chart. Another way to draw the map is to use a circle in the middle with connecting lines to the center. The lines can show connections of ideas to the center as well as connections among ideas.

Two Types of Cluster Map Designs

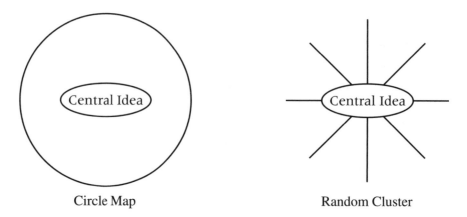

Circle Map   Random Cluster

Four cluster map techniques to use with beginning-level ELLs are questioning strategies, use of meaning sketches, color coding, and movable text clippings.

1. **Questioning strategies**. Beginning-level ELLs cannot respond adequately to open-ended questions such as, "What do we know about this character?" Nevertheless applying appropriate questioning strategies is essential for discussion. Samples of beginning-level questions are:
   * yes/no questions: "Is Peter Rabbit trapped?"
   * either/or questions: "Is Peter Rabbit trapped in a watering can or a basket?"
   * short-answer questions: "What is Peter Rabbit trapped in?"
   * call for gestures: "Point to the watering can where Peter Rabbit is trapped."

These types of questions invite the beginning ELL to respond according to ability level. The teacher follows by expanding and elaborating the students' responses and recording a more detailed phrase or complete sentence on the cluster map.

2. **Use of meaningful sketches**. Visual clues are needed with ELLs at all levels and particularly with beginners. Draw meaningful sketches on the cluster map to accompany phrases and sentences.

3. **Color coding**. Identify similar ideas and code them by marking each group of like ideas with a different color. This initiates the process of grouping sentences into paragraphs and foreshadows the use of a tree map graphic organizer.

4. **Movable text clippings**. Consider writing student comments on sticky notes or on separate cut squares of paper. Then place the clippings on the cluster map. This strategy facilitates grouping ideas and transferring them to a tree map. For students who are not writing as yet, movable text clippings allows them to manipulate text into meaningful categories.

Tree maps. The tree map works in consort with the cluster map. The cluster map is used to collect and record random ideas, while the tree map transfers those same ideas to organized categories.

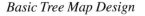

Basic Tree Map Design

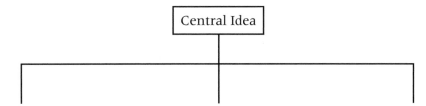

There are two ways to transfer ideas from the cluster map to the tree map. The first way uses the color-coding technique from the cluster map above. Each branch of the tree map corresponds to a color. Students copy the words on the branches according to color and then name the category. An alternative is to use the movable text clippings and simply have students pull them from the cluster map and arrange them in order on the branches of the tree map.

Once the tree map is completed, students can use it in a variety of ways. If the students are writing a single sentence, they can choose from a variety of phrases and sentences arranged on the tree. If they are writing a single paragraph, they can sample a sentence from each of the branches. If they are writing multiple paragraphs, they decide on the order of the branches and use a branch for the content of each paragraph.

Tip for parent involvement: Teach parents about the use of semantic maps. Even parents with limited levels of literacy can help their children organize their writing using simple maps. Teach them to expect the child to use a random cluster first, and then follow with a tree map before beginning to write in paragraph form.

Making collaborative big books. Making big books is a whole class project. There are five steps to the process.

Preparation

1. Materials: felt-tipped markers, chart paper, scissors, pencils, crayons or colored pencils, masking tape for binding.

2. Divide the class into pairs. Each pair will get one page of the big book, so you can figure the number of pages you will need according to the number of pairs, plus a cover page and a back page. (More elaborate big books will include a table of contents and authors' page.)

3. Crease chart paper in half. The number of the sheets is based on the number of pairs of students in your class (see #2 above). The folded sheet is a double-sided page. The folded edge is on the outside of the book; the open end is to be taped on the inside, or binding side, of the book.

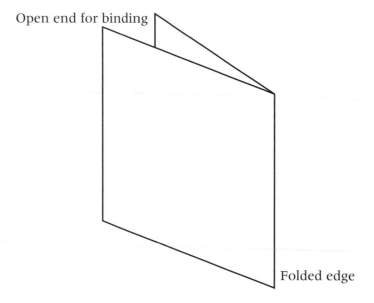

Open end for binding

Folded edge

Prewriting/Arranging

1. Establish a theme to write about. I recommend making a big book about a shared experience such as a recent field trip to the zoo, or a musical concert the class attended.

2. Ask each student to think of a sentence about the shared experience.

3. The teacher records each sentence on a sheet of chart paper for all to see. Avoid repeated ideas. Each sentence should be unique.

4. As a class, decide the order of the sentences from first to last. Number the sentences according to the order established by the students.

5. Slice sentences off of the chart. Use scissors to cut out each numbered sentence.

6. Ask students to sit with their partners.

Drafting/Illustrating

1. Paired students sit side by side. Give each pair of students a sheet of folded chart paper and two sequential sentence strips. Partner group A would get the first and second sentences, partner group B would get the third and fourth sentences, and so forth.

2. Depending on their writing ability, ask the students either to glue the sentence strip or copy it on their side of the folded sheet of paper.

3. Each student then illustrates their side of the paper.

Editing/Proofing

1. Students are responsible for checking their partner's page for accuracy, by comparing the writing against the original sentence strip.

2. The teacher double-checks each page.

3. Once both sides of the sheet are proofed, students may sign their work.

4. Ask students who have finished early to design and illustrate a book cover.

Binding

1. Binding the big book is a two-step process using masking tape. Order the book pages with the folded edges facing out and the open ends on the inside. Open the book as if it were bound and run a line of tape down the middle to bind sequential pages. The book will begin to look like a large accordion as the open, inside edges are taped together.

2. When all inside edges are taped together, close the book. Wrap masking tape around the edges to seal and hold the book together.

Publishing

1. Read the bound book to the whole class.

2. Keep the book on display for self-selected reading.

3. Keep it as a record of shared class experiences.

4. Check with the school librarian about making a section for classroom big books that can be checked out.

Tip for parent involvement: Ask parents to listen as their child reads a self-published book. Have parents ask the child to read individually to each member of the family to develop fluency and to motivate the child to be an author.

Triante poetry writing with beginners. Poetry writing is a way to express a personal experience, idea, or response to literature. With beginning-level students who speak using one- or two-word utterances, it is useful to provide a simple way to combine words to write a poem. A triante poem format is a triangular-shaped poem that is ideal for this purpose because students collaboratively compose a meaningful cascade of words that do not require attention to conventions of grammar and punctuation.

The writing process requires two scaffold techniques: use of a word bank and transferring selected words to a triante poetry frame. The process can be conducted as a group and then repeated for individual writing.

Prewriting

1. Begin with an experience such as a walk in a garden or selected place around the school.

2. As the students walk, make observations of what you encounter according to the senses of smell, sound, sight, and touch. Use taste only if the experience involves eating.

3. Create a word bank chart to list the words the students come up with under the appropriate sense category.

Triante Poem Word Bank (sample)

Smell	Sound	Sight	Touch
sweet	crackles	huge	fuzzy
like flowers	snaps	bright	soft
spice	whirring	blue	prickly
	hum	clear	smooth
			delicate

Drafting/Revision/Editing

1. Create a triante poem frame to guide drafting, revision, and editing of the poem.

Triante Poem Frame

_____

(Title)

_____ _____

(Smell: 2 words)

_____ _____ _____

(Sound: 3 words)

_____ _____ _____ _____

(Sight: 4 words)

_____ _____ _____ _____ _____

(Touch: 5 words)

2. Using the words that were recorded on the word bank chart, discuss which words should be transferred to the triante poem frame. Discuss selection, order of placement, and spelling and capitalization of each word for the poem. A sample triante poem follows.

Flower

Sweet spice

Hum crackle snaps

Clear blue bright huge

Delicate smooth soft fuzzy prickly

3. Once the words are written on the chart, students may either copy the poem or use the word bank to create their own individual triante poems.

Publish

1. Ask students to rewrite the chart without the drawn lines and word directives. Illustrate the large chart and display on a wall. Have all participants sign the poem.

2. Rewrite individual poems on colorful stationery, and display them on a bulletin board or bind them as a book of poems to make available in the classroom library or school library.

Tip for parent involvement: Ask parents to have the child rewrite the poem on stationery. Mail the poem to another member of the family to increase the audience for the published work.

Use this idea for any kind of shape poem, such as a diamond, circle, or hour-glass shape. The possibilities are endless. Each shape can use the same word bank configuration.

Interactive Writing Activities for Beginners

Interactive writing is defined here as writing between a novice and a more experienced writer. The interaction between the two writers creates a zone of proximal development which functions to mediate the development of writing proficiency. Moll (1997) refers to it as a literate and mediated relationship. The following activities are useful at each level of proficiency, but specific adaptive techniques are suggested in order to match the task to the ability level of the beginning English Language Learner.

Interactive journal writing. Interactive journal writing is a way to establish an instructional dialog in written form, with the more experienced writer modeling the language for the novice. The novice writer establishes the theme or content of the writing and the experienced writer models conventions of grammar, punctuation, and spelling. Just as reading with a child fosters fluency and comprehension, journal writing with a novice writer fosters fluency with written expression.

In terms of the writing process, journal writing is not intended to reach the publishing stage; therefore the focus is the initial draft in the journal. Revision and editing stages may not necessarily play a part in the process.

Preparation

1. Provide for each student a notebook, composition book, or a self-made journal with lined and unlined paper for writing and drawing.

2. Plan a time each day to write in journals. I suggest that students journal at the beginning of an instructional period, for example while attendance is being taken and homework collected, or after a recess so that the students know exactly what to do the moment they enter the classroom.

3. Allow ten to fifteen minutes for the journal writing time.

4. Display a sign with directions for journal writing:

Journal Writing

1. What to write about? Write about an event, experience, idea, or response to literature.

2. Spelling questions? Try your best guess; circle the word.

3. Don't know the word? Draw a picture.

4. Read your writing aloud to yourself, then read it to a partner or an adult before bringing it to the teacher.

Responding to Journals

1. Once students have taken time to write in their journals, the teacher or more experienced students respond in writing.

2. Respond to the content written in the journal. Avoid writing bland statement such as "nice writing." If the student writes "I like ice cream," respond with comments such as "I like ice cream too. My favorite flavor of ice cream is strawberry. What is your favorite?" Four techniques are at play here. First, maintain the same content in the response; second, write using many of the same words to model conventions; third, extend the theme with more details; and fourth, ask a question to evoke further written responses.

Managing Journal Writing

1. To avoid drowning in journal writing, don't respond to all journals every day. Consider the following suggestions:

   • If you have no helpers, ask students to write in journals for two or more days before you respond to them. Another approach is for students to write Mondays and Wednesdays, to give you two days to respond.

   • If you have parent volunteers, involve them in journal writing.

   • If you have cross-age tutors, train them to write to your students.

   • If you have students who are more experienced writers, designate them as respondents. Give respondents special pens to designate their role. Five respondents can easily write with four other students each to address 20 students total.

2. Organize the class according to a weekly journal-responding calendar. Divide up the class into four groups according to the days of the week. On Monday the teacher responds to group 1, on Tuesday to group 2, and so forth. Leave Fridays open to catch up on students who were absent during the week.

3. Color-code the journals for the day of the week you respond to: for example, red journals on Mondays, blue on Tuesdays, green on Wednesdays, and purple on Thursdays. This facilitates collecting and returning

journals. Designate a student from each color group to collect and distribute the completed journals. Store the journals in colored baskets that match their color group.

Lap board model writing. Some essential tools for modeling interactive writing are a small white board with a dry erase marker and eraser, and white correctional tape. Use these tools when developing charts with students.

Procedure

1. When writing a chart story or filling in a word bank, invite the students to write the words. To help the student write conventionally, hold a white board up and ask the other students watching how to spell the key words. Model conventional spelling in dialog with the students. Point out the features of the word as you write it on the board.

2. If the student makes a mistake while writing on a chart in front of the class, provide white correctional tape. Allow the student to cover the misspelling and rewrite the correct word over the taped section.

Individual Writing Activities for Beginners

Individual writing opportunities are limited for beginning-level students. In order for these students to write individually, they must be given the opportunity to visually represent their ideas in a nonverbal way with pictures, such as pictorial journals and personal illustrated books.

Pictorial journals for individual expression. A pictorial journal is a collage of drawings and pasted pictures that represent the weekly events, experiences, and thoughts in a child's life. But it is more than pictures; with assistance, words are also incorporated to facilitate individual writing.

Preparation

1. Provide each student with a three-ring, loose-leaf binder.

2. Collect pictures cut from periodicals. Store and maintain the picture collection in a box.

3. Supply each student with a three-hole-punched piece of paper with a large space for pictures and lines for writing at the bottom of the page. Date the page for the current week.

4. Provide colored pencils or crayons for drawing and glue for pasting.

5. Develop and maintain a bulletin board with high-frequency words to assist in sentence building.

Procedure

1. Schedule time every other day to draw or select pictures from the picture box that represent the student's experience, allowing a day for glue to dry before the picture is placed in a binder.

2. While students are selecting, gluing, and drawing pictures, move from student to student. Ask them, what is in the picture? Label the pictures or drawings with the appropriate names.

3. The next day that pictorial journals are worked on, ask students to use the labeled words to write about the collage they have created.

4. Encourage students to use the high-frequency words on the bulletin board word wall to put together the picture words into complete sentences.

5. Completed pages are placed in the loose-leaf binder. Over time, the pictorial journal will give evidence of writing growth.

Tip for parent involvement: Make parents active participants in journal writing on a weekly basis. Encourage them to write their comments in the child's journal. In the case that the parent is illiterate, ask an older sibling to write what the parent dictates, and read the entry aloud to the parent.

Making personal illustrated books. Fundamental to writing a story is to sequence story events. For the beginning-level student who may not be able to write more than a few words, making personal illustrated books is a first step in crossing the bridge from solely producing oral language to using print. Drawing story events is the key to making a personal illustrated book. The following directions show how to assist beginning ELLs in making personal illustrated books.

1. Provide the student with a storyboard frame.

Title_____ Author and Illustrator_____ Date_____	(1)	(2)	(3)
(4)	(5)	(6)	(7)

2. Demonstrate how to draw a sequence of events to tell a story. Use a familiar storybook as a model.

3. Ask the students to draw their own stories in sequence. Suggest that they illustrate a story from their own lives. Encourage them to interview their parents or other family members about an important event in their family's experience.

4. When the storyboard is complete, help the student formulate a title. They write their own name in as author/illustrator. Date the storyboard on the title page.

5. Use scissors to cut the storyboard into individual frames.

6. Collate the pieces into sequential order with the title page on top.

7. Staple at the end to bind the book.

Students can use the book to talk about a significant experience in their lives. An adult or cross-age tutor can write the words on the book pages to give the students practice in reading about themselves. The storyboard format also prepares students for organizing writing and presentations using software such as PowerPoint.

Early Intermediate and Intermediate Level

Students at early intermediate and intermediate levels of proficiency are able to write simple sentences and paragraphs. Even though they are able to address conventions of grammar, spelling, and punctuation, students at this level require extensive scaffolding with word banks, writing frames, and graphic organizers. While collaborative, interactive, and individual writing employ all of these kinds of scaffolds, the way they are applied varies with the purpose of the writing project.

Collaborative Writing Activities for Early Intermediate and Intermediate Levels

Collaborative poetry writing. This section addresses three forms of poetry writing that are appropriate for students at the early intermediate and intermediate levels of proficiency: haiku, cinquain, and biopoems. As with the triante poem, there are two components: the word bank and the poetry frame. The design of the word bank and frame is dictated by the specific poetry form, but the writing process for each is essentially the same.

Haiku. Haiku is a Japanese poetry form. There are no hard and fast rules regarding this simplified, children's version of haiku, but it does have several unique features. In Japanese, it is a seventeen-character poetry form, while in English it is a seventeen-syllable form. The syllables generally are arranged in three lines, consisting of five, seven, and five syllables, respectively. The theme is usually nature, but can deal with other areas. Haiku often finishes with a comical or ironic ending.

Prewriting

1. Begin by practicing forming phrases with five or seven syllables.

2. Create an experience such as a nature walk.

3. As the students walk, make observations of what you encounter according to the senses. They are to think about how to express their sensations in five- or seven-syllable phrases.

4. Create a word bank chart in a T-table format to list their phrases (see sample below).

Haiku Poem Word Bank (sample)

5 Syllables	7 Syllables
the lotus flower	floating by the river bank
it smells like perfume	soft and delicate petals
frogs like to see them	decorating the water
bouncing with ripples	bugs are crawling around them
touching the surface	growing in pools of delight
wanting a bouquet	

Drafting/Revision/Editing

1. Create a haiku poetry frame to guide drafting, revision, and editing of the poem as a group:

_____

(5 syllables)

_____

(7 syllables)

_____

(5 syllables)

2. Using the words that were recorded on the word bank chart, discuss which words should be transferred to the poetry frame. Discuss selection, order of placement, and spelling and capitalization of each word for the poem. Write the resulting haiku in the poetry frame, for example:

the lotus flower

decorating the water

wanting a bouquet

3. Once the poem is written, students may either copy it or use the word bank to create their own individual haiku poems.

Publish

1. Ask students to rewrite the chart poem without the drawn lines and word directives. Illustrate the large chart and display on a wall. Have all participants sign the poem.

2. Rewrite individual poems on colorful stationery, display on a bulletin board, or bind as a book of poems to make available in the classroom library or in the school library.

Cinquain. Cinquain comes from the French work *cinq*, meaning "five." It is a five-line poem that utilizes the same format of a word bank and a frame. In this case, the word bank requires words that are adjectives, verbs, and adverbs. This presents a contextual way to teach parts of speech.

Cinquain Word Bank

Describing Words *(Adjectives)*	*Action Words* *(Verbs)*	*Feeling Words* *(Adverbs)*

Cinquain Poetry Frame

_____

(Title)

_____

(3 describing words—adjectives)

_____

(3 action words—verbs)

_____

(3 feeling words—adverbs)

_____

(Refers to title)

Biopoems. Biopoems are a poetic way to describe one's self. The word bank is slightly more complex, but the process is the same. An alternate way to use a biopoem is to apply the format to a character study as literary response and analysis. This only works well if the character being studied is very rich and there is information about parentage and aspirations.

Biopoem Word Bank

Descriptors	*Lover of . . .*	*Who feels . . .*	*Who needs . . .*	*Would like to see . . .*

Biopoem Frame

First Name _____

4 words that tell about you (or a story character)

_____ _____ _____ _____

Child of _____

Lover of (3 things) _____ _____ _____

Who feels (3 feelings) _____ _____ _____

Who needs (3 ideas) _____ _____ _____

Who would like to see (3 things)_____ _____ _____

Resident of _____

Last Name _____

Collaborative songwriting. The combination of melody, rhythm, and verse appear to make sense to people with a certain ability in music, but to many, songwriting is a mysterious process. There is a simple way to involve children collaboratively in writing songs. If you borrow a familiar tune, you no longer need to compose melody and rhythm. What is left to do is manipulate the text so that it fits the melody. This is done by the same format of using an appropriately designed word bank and a song frame. With songs, the word bank and song frame are designed to accommodate the syllable count of each line of the song. It operates just the same way as the haiku poem word bank and frame.

The following songwriting activities use four familiar melodies with accompanying word banks and song frames. The writing process is essentially the same as the poetry sequence described above. The familiar melodies are "Are You Sleeping," "London Bridge," "Twinkle, Twinkle Little Star," and a blues favorite by Jimmy Reed, "You Got Me Up, You Got Me Down." I will describe the writing process for "Are You Sleeping" and then list the other word bank and song frames.

Prewriting

1. Practice forming phrases with four, three, and six counts.

2. Refer to a theme or an experience such as a story, or shared experience such as a field trip.

3. Elicit phrases from students in either four, three, or six syllables.

4. Create a word bank chart to list their phrases as either four, three, or six syllable counts. Note that the order of the chart matches the order of the song frame with the first line of the song being four syllables.

"Are You Sleeping" Word Bank

4 Syllables	*3 Syllables*	*6 Syllables*

Drafting/Revision/Editing

1. Compose a song using a frame to guide drafting, revision, and editing of the lyrics as a group.

"Are You Sleeping" Song Frame

_____

(Title)

_____

(4 syllables)

_____

(4 syllables)

_____

(3 syllables)

_____

(3 syllables)

_____

(6 syllables)

_____

(6 syllables)

_____

(3 syllables)

_____

(3 syllables)

2. Using the words that were recorded on the word bank chart, discuss which words should be transferred to the song frame. Discuss selection, order of placement, and spelling and capitalization of each word for the song.

3. Once the words are written on the song frame, students may either copy the lyrics or use the word bank to create their own individual songs.

Publish

1. Ask students to rewrite the chart song without the drawn lines and word directives. Illustrate the large chart and display on a wall. Have all participants sign the song.

2. Rewrite individual songs on colorful stationery, display on a bulletin board, or bind as a song book to make available in the classroom library or in the school library.

3. Sing the songs together as a class. A song such as "Are You Sleeping" can be sung as a round.

Other Collaborative Song Word Banks and Frames

"Twinkle, Twinkle Little Star" Word Bank

4 Syllables	*3 Syllables*

"Twinkle, Twinkle Little Star" Song Frame

_____

(Title)

_____

(4 syllables)

_____

(3 syllables)

_____

(4 syllables)

_____

(3 syllables)

_____

(4 syllables)

_____

(3 syllables)

_____

(4 syllables)

_____

(3 syllables)

_____

(4 syllables)

_____

(3 syllables)

_____

(4 syllables)

_____

(3 syllables)

"London Bridge" Word Bank

4 Syllables	3 Syllables	2 Syllables

"London Bridge" Song Frame

_____

(Title)

_____

(4 syllables)

_____

(3 syllables)

_____

(3 syllables)

_____

(3 syllables)

_____

(4 syllables)

_____

(3 syllables)

_____

(2 syllables)

_____

(2 syllables)

"You Got Me Up, You Got Me Down" Blues Word Bank

4 Syllables	3 Syllables	2 Syllables	6 Syllables	9 Syllables

"You Got Me Up, You Got Me Down" Song Frame

_____

(Title)

_____

(4 syllables)

_____

(4 syllables)

_____

(3 syllables)

_____

(2 syllables)

_____

(2 syllables)

_____

(6 syllables)

_____

(3 syllables)

_____

(3 syllables)

_____

(9 syllables)

_____

(9 syllables)

Interactive Writing Activities for Early Intermediate and Intermediate Levels

Writing interactively at the early intermediate and intermediate levels includes longer passages and can also involve family members and pen pals. Family journal writing is a five-day cycle of writing that establishes a routine for developing individual writing. Pen pals is not a new idea, but the organization and delivery techniques may prove helpful.

Tip for parent involvement: Use the following activity as a means to create a family treasure. Use a large composition book with more than 100 pages to maintain the family journal throughout the entire school year. The child and the parents will cherish this journal for years.

Interactive family journal writing. Inviting the family to participate in journal writing recognizes that literacy begins at home. In some cases the parents may not be able to participate due to low literacy levels in the home language. In that case, the student is encouraged to invite another adult or an older sibling to participate. The graphic organizer techniques used in this activity are described earlier in the chapter.

The following is a five-day journal writing cycle that involves family members. At the beginning of the school year, the teacher will want to model each step explicitly. Once the routine is established, the activity will operate virtually automatically as a regular part of the classroom work.

Five-Day Family Journal Writing Cycle

Day 1: On the first page of the journal, make a circle map to brainstorm journal-entry ideas.

Day 2: Transfer the random ideas on the circle map to a simple tree map.

Day 3: Write one or more paragraphs based on the tree map.

Day 4: Take home to read it to an adult. The adult writes a response and poses a question.

Day 5: The child responds to the adult's question. Teacher reads the week's journal entries and posts a comment with a sticky note.

Our family participated in such a cycle with a journal in Spanish. Here is our daughter Kathryn's third-grade journal.

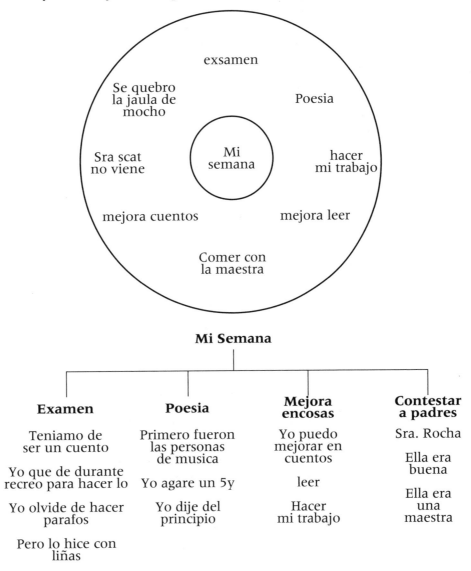

12/2/01
fecha

Querida Mama:

Mi semana era buena. Mi mejor susituta era Sra. Rocha. Ella era mi susituta mas favorito porque, era una buena susituta hablaba español y porque ella era una maestra. Si guste el libro.

Teniamos un exsamen. Teniamos que hacer un cuento. Yo hice de cuando ayude a Corrine en el reporte. Yo no sabia para escribir y quede para recreo y agare una idea. Cuando estaba escridiendo olvide de hacer parafo pero lo ise con liñas.

Isimo la poesa diferente esta semana. Las personas que tenian clase de musica fueron primeros y las personas que no fuero depues. Si dices toda la poema del principio agaras una ☆ y el otro numero que agarastes. Yo agare un 5 y ☆. Lo dije el principio.

Ahora voy a dicir de las cosas que puedo mejoran en, como contar cuentos mejor. Recordar de hacer parafos. Leer y entender que estoy leendo. Algo muy importante es hacer mi trabajo y terminarlo.

Con cariño,
Kathryn

---

el 3 de diciembre 2001

Querida Kathryn,

Ayer me viste llorar. Lloraba porque estaba tratando de expresar mis sentimientos por la directora pre-escolar de Woods-Edgewater que está jubilandose. Tiene que jubilarse porque está muy enferma con cancer. No sabemos si va a vivir en algunos meses. Señorita Betty Woods era una mujer sumamente ejemplar. Ayudaba a muchos niños y sus padres. Dime algo,

☆¿Qué recuerdos tienes de Señorita Betty?
☆¿Qué aprendiste de ella?

Con mucho cariño,
Daddy

Interactive writing with pen pals. Pen pals are pairs of students who commit to corresponding with each other. Two primary considerations dictate the management of pen pals. Are the pen pals local at the school site? Or are they separated by a considerable distance? With pen pals at the same school site, a correspondence center can be created and maintained to facilitate the writing and distribution of the letters. With distant pen pals, consider establishing an "email pals" system.

Local school-site pen pals are easy to set up and maintain.

1. Make a connection with another class at your school that would be willing to partici-pate in a pen pals project.
2. Make a mailbag. Decorate a canvas, two-handle bag with the name of the school and the words "Mail Carrier for Room # ____" (Fill in your classroom's room number).

Designate a classroom "Mail Carrier(s)" to deliver mail daily or every other day. Hang the mailbag by the door of the classroom for easy access.

3. Create a correspondence center: a small portable file box labeled "Correspondence Center" that can be easily stored on a shelf when not in use. Place the following items in the file box:
   - File folders labeled with the students' names, one on each folder
   - A materials folder with stationery and envelopes
   - A cup with pens
   - A laminated card with letter-writing format on one side and mailing directions on the other side
   - A laminated map of the school with room numbers noted

4. On the front of the laminated card, display a standard "friendly" letter-writing format as follows:

```
                                              (YOUR FULL NAME)
                                              (CLASSROOM ADDRESS)


        (DATE)
        (GREETING) Dear _____,
        (BODY OF THE LETTER)

        _____

        _____

        _____

        _____


                                              (CLOSING) Sincerely,
                                              (SIGNATURE)
```

On the opposite side of the laminated card, outline the pen pal procedure and guidelines.
- Write a friendly letter to your designated pen pal
- Before putting your letter in an envelope, check to make sure you have each component of the letter in place. Did you write your name and classroom address?
- Write your pen pal's name and the classroom number on the front of the envelope.
- Place the letter in the mailbag for the next delivery.

Email pal sites allow students to correspond with students around the world. Setting up email pals is safe and easy with Web-based connection sites. Basically, a Web-based connection site provides the conduit for sending email, matches students according to profiles, and allows correspondents to select the language for writing. One consideration with using a Web-based connection site is that it comes with a nominal price. The following are two Web-based connection sites.

www.epals.com ePALS Classroom Exchange is designed to work with school programs. It offers teachers and students a world-wide, safe, monitored, multilingual email pal system.

A unique feature of the site is that it is developed in compliance with "No Child Left Behind" (NCLB) federal guidelines. Compliance includes parent involvement, seamless education K–16, teacher projects, and Internet safety tips. The program, established in 1976, has safely operated with child participation for almost 30 years. Furthermore, the site is easy to navigate.

www.world-pen-pals.com World Pen Pals is not exclusively for school programs. Originally developed for traditional correspondence over fifty years ago, it offers multiple language correspondence with a secure, monitored system. Picture exchanges are only permitted with participants who are eighteen and older.

Individual Writing Activities for Early Intermediate and Intermediate Levels

Virtually any form of writing can be produced on an individual basis. Although early intermediate and intermediate ELLs are limited in what they can do individually, they can engage in a wide range of writing activities if given scaffolded writing frames. Two activities that are appropriate for this level are double-entry journals and expository writing frames.

Double-entry journals. Double-entry journals are designed to reference reflections, to tie one's reflections to a specific idea or passage in a book. Double-entry journals are composed of a two-column page. In the left column, the writer notes a reference statement. The reference statement could be a title for an idea, a label of a thought, or a citation from a book. In the right column, the writer expands on the idea or reference with a reflective comment.

Double-entry journals are particularly useful for literary response. Students can reference a specific character trait, event, or thought and then write about their perceptions and understandings of the passage. The practice of noting references and citations and then writing a reflective comment is a valuable skill for exploring and recalling one's ideas. It also is a contextual way to teach students note-taking strategies. Below is a format for double-entry journals.

Double-Entry Journal

Name _____		Date_____
Reading Selection _____		No. of Pages _____
References/Citations		*Reflections*

Expository writing frame. Expository writing is standard practice for academic writing. Students need to be proficient in the format to organize topical writing. Intermediate students writing about topics in content areas will benefit from the use of a writing frame for a standard five-paragraph expository essay.

The standard five-paragraph essay employs specific features including a topic sentence highlighting the main points of the essay, transitional sentences leading the reader from one idea to the next, and a conclusion summarizing the ideas discussed in the body of the essay. Below is a frame that can be used to help students organize their expository writing.

Expository Writing Frame

Paragraph #1	Topic sentence: Idea A: Idea B: Idea C:

Paragraph #2	Expand idea A: Transition sentence:

Paragraph #3	Expand idea B: Transition sentence:

Paragraph #4	Expand idea C: Transition sentence:

Paragraph #5	Conclusion (summarize ideas A, B, & C):

Early Advanced and Advanced Level

Writing at the early advanced and advanced levels incorporates a full range of writing activities. Students at this level write at grade level and often above grade level proficiency due to the fact that they have intentionally and explicitly developed English to a high degree. They also have the advantage of drawing on their own linguistic and cultural diversity which gives them a more complex understanding of their words and their world.

What distinguishes an advanced ELL writer from a native English writer is that there will still be the occasional gap in use of the language that needs to be taught explicitly. Some of the gaps a teacher can anticipate are new vocabulary in specific content areas and/or changes in literary style such as the shift from expository to persuasive writing. This does not limit early advanced or advanced students' writing capacity. What it means is that the teacher needs to be vigilant for the gaps and prepared to address them. When introducing a new concept, the discipline-specific vocabulary must be taught first. Checking for prior knowledge before teaching a new writing style by asking students to paraphrase concepts in their own words is a way to anticipate needed instruction.

Activities for students at advanced levels include refining the use of language, larger writing projects, and more complex forms of writing. Collaborative activities include developing metaphorical thinking with similes in a song, and team writing in which students work on larger projects such as edited collections or newsletters. Interactive writing still includes using journals in formats discussed previously, but students can engage in asynchronous dialog on on-line discussion boards. Individual writing projects increase in complexity and demand that the student offer a critique, state an opinion, or persuade an audience.

Collaborative Writing Activities for Early Advanced and Advanced Levels

Singing similes. "Mr. MacGregor's Garden" is a song I wrote for a group of students to play with the use of simile. The words are easy and the song creates a frame for metaphorical thinking.

Procedure: Sing through the song as a group. Sing through the chorus, "Mr. MacGregor had a very funny garden . . .", a second time. When you get to the verse, "And he grew . . .", call on students to insert fruits or vegetables and state what the color or texture is. Then ask them to make a metaphorical comparison or simile.

Once the group gets the feel for the song, get imaginative. See what ideas and similes the group can come up with that one would not expect to find in a garden. For example, "And he grew snow tires, spiked snow tires. Snow tires as spiked as a porcupine. . . ."

Mr. MacGregor's Garden

by Dr.BB

Mr. MacGregor had a very funny garden,

a very funny garden,

a very funny garden,

Mr. MacGregor had a very funny garden,

and he worked in it all day long.

And he grew lettuce, green lettuce

Lettuce as green as fresh cut grass

And he grew tomatoes, red tomatoes

Tomatoes as red as a fire truck.

And he grew __(fruit or vegetable)__, __(color or texture)__ __(fruit or vegetable)__ __(fruit or vegetable)__ as __(color or texture)__ as __(simile)__

And he grew __(fruit or vegetable)__, __(color or texture)__ __(fruit or vegetable)__ __(fruit or vegetable)__ as __(color or texture)__ as __(simile)__

Team writing with larger projects. Team writing projects are for larger works. They can take various forms such as edited collections of writing, newsletters, or content area group reports. They also may be used for media-based productions such as a video-magazine program.

With the team concept, there are several shifts to note in terms of roles and the writing process. First of all, the role of the teacher shifts from the source of information and assignments to that of publisher. The publisher outlines general guidelines, and reviews, monitors, and evaluates the work. The students assume more autonomy with regard to writing assignments, working like an editorial board. As a team, students develop their own projects within the guidelines established by the teacher. They must develop an initial concept and present it in the form of a proposal. They also monitor and edit their own work. This approach expands the writing process, adding a proposal development component within the prewriting stage.

Although the final, written products will vary greatly, the writing team roles remain constant from project to project: the teacher is executive editor, and students take on roles of managing editor, design and layout editor, copy editor, or contributing writer. All team members share in the work as copy editors and contributing writers. This ensures that each student is held responsible to attend to writing conventions and to produce a written piece. No one is allowed to avoid writing and editing text with this rule in place. Each member's role is described in Table 7.2 within the framework of the team.

Even though each team member has one or more specific roles in the writing process, all members are evaluated. Evaluation of the students' writing takes place on two levels: the quality of the whole project, and the individual contributions of each team member. The evaluation is discussed below in the procedure for the Team Writing Process.

Team Writing Process

Prewriting

1. Guidelines for writing and publishing may vary according to the specific project. The teacher presents guidelines in accordance with content standards and genre. (See rubric language guidelines below in the assessment section.)

2. Writing team recruitment and development should be done initially by the teacher. Once the students understand the process, they can take initiative and form their own teams. The teacher may want to consider guidelines for gender equity, for example, that each team must be made up of equal numbers of boys and girls. Once teams are formed, members decide which roles they will assume.

3. Proposal development requires the use of a Team Writing Proposal Form (see sample). The students decide on a working title, assign themselves to editorial roles, briefly describe the project idea, and present an outline with assigned authors, a calendar for the process, and a list of resources and materials needed.

4. Proposal review is conducted by the teacher. In the right-hand column of the Team Writing Proposal Form, there is a place for inserting comments and providing approval for each part of the project. This is where the teacher monitors who is doing what task and the feasibility of the project. The teacher also verifies if the project meets the established guidelines. Before a project can be started, each component of the proposal must obtain prior approval.

5. Proposal revision and resubmission for review may be required. This is a recursive process. A team may need to rework all or part of a proposal and resubmit it for review. Attention to details and the anticipation of problems at this point can save a writing team hours of work.

TABLE 7.2   *Team Writing Roles and Responsibilities*

Roles	Responsibilities
Teacher: Publisher	• Teach team project writing process • Outline writing and publishing guidelines • Assign or recruit managing editors • Consult on and evaluate project proposals • Monitor team writing process • Acquire equipment and materials • Evaluate individual contributions • Evaluate final project
Managing editor(s)	• Act as liaison to the teacher • Recruit team members • Chair team writing meetings • Lead initial concept and proposal development • Ensure consistent project focus • Authorize inclusion of submissions • Handle requests for materials • Write the introduction of the project • Copy editor • Contributing writer
Design and layout editor(s)	• Computer input and organization of writing selections • Merge document files of individual submissions into larger project • Ensure consistent layout of font and formats • Select and edit cover art • Select and edit graphics (clip art, cartoons, icons, maps, illustrations) • Copy editor • Contributing writer
Copy editor(s) **(All team members)**	• Review drafts of writing for conventions of spelling, grammar, and punctuation • Review writing to ensure that the themes and content are consistent with the focus of the larger work • Ensure consistent writing style • Copy editor • Contributing writer
Contributing writers **(All team members)**	• Get a writing assignment from managing editor • Draft writing consistent with the proposal guidelines • Revise drafts • Submit writing as a word-processed document • Copy editor for another contributing writer

Team Writing Proposal Form

Project Working Title	**Publisher's Comments**
	Approved? Y/N
Team Members Managing Editor(s): Design and Layout Editor(s): Copy Editor(s): Contributing Editor(s):	 Approved? Y/N
Brief Description of the Project (*What's the big idea?*)	 Approved? Y/N
Proposed Outline (*List headings and name each author*) I. II. III. IV. V.	 Approved? Y/N
Writing Process Calendar *Deadlines*	
Initial drafts Due date: Revised drafts Due date: Computer design/layout Due date: Final revisions Due date: Submit as published Due date:	 Approved? Y/N
Resources and Materials Needed • • • • • •	 Approved? Y/N

Draft

1. An editorial board meeting of the entire team is convened by the managing editor once the proposal is approved. The purpose of the meeting is to review the proposal and publisher comments and to distribute writing assignments and set deadlines for first drafts.

2. Each member of the writing team contributes a piece to be included in the project. Specific guidelines about content and length are clarified at the editorial board meeting.

Revise

1. The editorial board meets again to check writing progress. Agenda items for the meeting may include problems encountered with the original assignments, formatting considerations and fonts, and artwork and graphics to include. Check source material and citations.

2. Each writer shares work and listens to the comments of the group. Changes are suggested and the next deadline for the writing is established.

3. The team provides the managing editor with essential content for writing the introduction to the project.

Edit

1. The editorial board meets for the purpose of reviewing revised drafts for conventions of spelling, grammar, and punctuation.

2. Each member of the team functions as a copy editor at this stage. It is recommended that they all review the writing of each group member so that it gets a maximum number of reviews.

3. Check for placement of graphics and edit cover art.

Publish

1. Format each file with the same fonts and styles.

2. Merge each document file into the one file.

3. Insert graphics and apply cover art.

4. Print out hard copies of the work.

5. Compile, bind, and present to the class for display.

Evaluation

1. Individual contributions are evaluated by a self-evaluation and a rubric evaluation of the writing. The self-evaluation is written by each team member describing what was written and other group responsibilities (see sample form). Rubric assessment language is provided at the end of this chapter.

Self-Evaluation of Team Writing

Your Name:	Date:
Project Title:	
Role: ____ Managing Editor _____ Design and Layout Editor ____ Copy Editor ____ Contributing Writer	
What was your strongest contribution?	
In what area did you need the most help?	
What was the best part of the project?	
How would you do the project differently?	

2. Entire project evaluation is done using a rubric that is established in the guidelines at the beginning of the process. Essentially the rubric evaluates the project as a whole for conventions and content. Each team member receives an individual and a group grade.

Interactive Writing Activities for Early Advanced and Advanced Levels

To increase the level of depth and complexity of interactive writing for early advanced and advanced English Language Learners, consider using asynchronous dialog on on-line discussion boards, also known in the vernacular as newsgroups.

Discussion boards. Discussion boards, or newsgroups, are a Web-based way to invite writing dialog about a particular subject. A teacher or group leader posts a message as a prompt. Participants respond directly to the prompt or to another participant's comments.

The string of messages related to a single prompt is called a thread. The term asynchronous dialog describes the way the threads are formed. They do not develop in a linear fashion. A contributor may make an initial comment in response to the prompt and then scroll through the other messages to find an interesting one to respond to.

Caution is advised here. Only engage in discussion boards with children if you have a closed on-line system. Closed on-line systems are course suites designed specifically for classroom use. The site is only available to instructors and students that have been enrolled in the course. A quick search of Web sites that offer discussion boards or newsgroups will tell you that open on-line systems have few safety controls built-in for child protection. A closed network for classroom use is supplied by Web sites such as www.coursecompass.com and www.blackboard.com.

Individual Writing Activities for Early Advanced and Advanced Levels

Early advanced and advanced ELLs should write in a wide range of genres. Numerous forms of writing have already been discussed in this chapter and ELLs at this level can participate in all of them to a greater degree of depth and complexity than those at earlier levels. One form of writing that requires multiple skills is persuasive writing.

Persuasive writing. Persuasive writing, done well, demands evidence and well-reasoned arguments. Building a persuasive writing piece can be a recursive process that calls the writer to revise initial assumptions. A writer begins with an initial opinion, but then sets about to find evidence to support the opinion. Sometimes, after examining the evidence, a writer will change his mind and then become compelled to revise the original opinion.

A "Persuasive Writing Builder" is a format that allows for a recursive process (see sample below). The builder is used in the prewriting stage of the writing process. The balance of the writing would follow a standard writing process format.

1. Write a question that calls for an opinion. Although not the only way to form a question, yes/no and either/or questions do force an opinion. Sample questions would be, "Is chocolate bad for you?" or "Is chocolate good or bad for you?"
2. State an initial opinion. The initial opinion, at this point, gives the writer a direction; it does not have to be fully developed.

3.   Research the opinion. Cite the source for each piece of evidence. Note the following in the citation: Author (year), "Title of cited work." Page numbers. City, State: Publisher.
4.   Formulate an argument from each piece of evidence. Use phrases such as: "According to . . ." or "Based on . . ." or "Recent studies show . . ."
5.   Decide which argument is the strongest. In the "Argument" box, circle A for the strongest argument, B for the next strongest, and C for the least strong argument. This will determine the order of the paragraphs in the persuasive essay.
6.   Evaluate your initial opinion. Based on the evidence and the arguments, did the initial opinion change?
7.   If so, rewrite the opinion in the final box. If not, keep the initial opinion and begin drafting the persuasive writing piece. Consider revising the opinion to make it stronger.

Persuasive Writing Builder

Write a Yes/No or an Either/Or Question	
State Initial Opinion (What do you think?)	
Source: Evidence:	Argument: Order: [A B C]
Source: Evidence:	Argument: Order: [A B C]
Source: Evidence:	Argument: Order: [A B C]
Evaluate: Did your initial opinion change? Yes? or No? (If yes, rewrite the opinion below.)	
Revised Opinion:	

Writing Assessment Across Levels of Proficiency

The purpose of assessment is to evaluate growth of what students know and are able to do, and to report progress to the student, the family, and the educational support community. Part and parcel with assessment is the need to make adjustments in the instruction to match the assessed strengths and needs of the students. Teachers build on identified strengths and address specific needs with instruction.

A number of assessment tools are useful for writing. Below the writing assessment tools are listed according to appropriateness for proficiency levels. At the beginning level, the chart rubrics and journal assessment logs will be useful tools because they record growth over time and involve the students in assessing their own writing from the outset. More complex rubrics and writing conference record sheets are more helpful for students as they begin to demonstrate longer paragraph writing at the intermediate and advanced levels. Each of the assessment tools is helpful for advanced students. At the end of this chapter you will find rubric language for developing rubrics across levels of proficiency and across selected genres of writing.

Writing Assessment	*Beginning*	*Early Intermediate and Intermediate*	*Early Advanced and Advanced*
Tools	• Chart rubric • Journal assessment log	(Same as prior level) • Line item rubrics • Writing conference record sheets	(Same as prior level) • Rubric partners • Self-generated rubrics

Writing Assessment Tools Appropriate for Beginning English Language Learners

Chart rubric. A chart rubric is a displayed rubric to inform and remind students of the level of writing that they are to attain. Chart rubrics can take essentially two forms. One form displays generic criteria for writing in rubric form. The chart functions like a checklist of the highest level of attainment and usually only addresses conventions.

In Your Writing, Did You . . . ?

- Indent all paragraphs
- Write complete sentences
- Use ending punctuation
- Spell all words correctly

A much more powerful way to use a chart rubric is to display writing exemplars at each level. The exemplars are actual children's writing samples, enlarged for easy viewing, that exhibit the criteria for each grading level. A grading level is commonly a four-point scale, with 4 representing the highest level and 1 representing the lowest level. The powerful element of this idea is that students will compare their work to the exemplar chart to make their own assessment. When students begin to assess their own work against exemplary work, they become self-directed in addressing their own needs.

How to develop an exemplars chart rubric. Selecting exemplars takes a certain amount of work ahead of time.

1. Meet with teachers at your grade level.

2. Ask each teacher to a bring a range of student writing samples to evaluate.
3. Separate the student writing samples into graded levels of 1 to 4.
4. As a norming process, come to consensus on what a paper will look like at each level.
5. Select an anchor paper for each level as an exemplar. Often the most difficult one to find is the level 4 paper without errors. If you cannot identify a level 4 paper, consider utilizing a paper from the next grade level up to challenge students to improve their writing.
6. Obtain written permission from the parents of the children to use their papers for exemplars. Specify that the papers will be used anonymously.
7. Photocopy each exemplar in large format for easy display and viewing.
8. Mount the exemplars on a large strip of butcher paper according to their graded level.

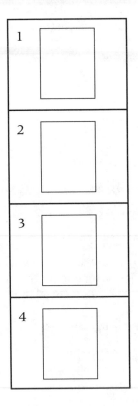

Journal assessment log. Once a month, ask students to write a journal entry for assessment purposes. Instead of writing the entry in the bound composition book or notebook, provide the students with a separate piece of paper which will be collected for assessment.

Use the journal assessment rubric (Table 7.3) to assess the journal writing for punctuation, structure, and grammar and syntax. It is recommended, due to the complex nature of the assessment, to check levels of developmental spelling twice during the school year. Note that content is not assessed in the journals due to the wide variety of topics and material that may be included in a journal.

Some classrooms have a bulletin board on which each student has a place to display the current month's evaluated journal entries. Over time, the journals will show growth and the display will be a way to communicate that growth to the student, family members, and the educational support community.

TABLE 7.3 *Rubric for Journal Assessment*

Journal Assessment	4	3	2	1
Punctuation (. , ? ! ; : ")	No errors, full usage of punctuation marks	Few errors, most punctuation evident	Many errors with some ending punctuation	Few to no punctuation marks used
Structure (Paragraphs and sentence)	Multiple, indented paragraphs with complete sentences	At least one indented paragraph with complete sentences	1 to 2 sentences, no indentation	Random words or letters with pictures
Grammar and Syntax • Noun/verb agreement • Preposition usage • Word order	No errors	Few errors	Many errors	No grammar or syntax evident
Spelling (*See chapter 4 for an assessment*)	Conventional	Transitional	Phonetic	Semiphonetic

Journal Assessment Log

Student Roster	Sept	Oct*	Nov	Dec	Jan	Feb	Mar*	Apr	May	June
1.										
2.										
3.										
4.										
5.										
6.										
7.										
8.										
9.										
10.										

(continued)

Student Roster	Sept	Oct*	Nov	Dec	Jan	Feb	Mar*	Apr	May	June
11.										
12.										
13.										
14.										
15.										
16.										
17.										
18.										
19.										
20.										

* In October and March check for levels of developmental spelling (see Chapter 4).

Writing Assessment Tools Appropriate for Early Intermediate and Intermediate English Language Learners

At the early-intermediate level and above, writing rubrics should address conventions of writing and the content of the writing, as well. Some rubric formats can be cumbersome to manage and difficult to use for assessment, but there is a simple way to address both conventions and content with line-item rubrics. Another assessment tool to use with students who are writing longer and more complex pieces is a writing conference log. The writing conference log records the essential information about a piece of writing and can be used for assessment data. Both tools are described below.

Line-item rubrics. Think of the times that you have seen student writing that had some wonderful ideas, but was seriously flawed by errors of punctuation, grammar, or spelling. Conversely, think of the writing that appears to be flawless, but is missing the content or lacks any substance.

The way to address both conventions and content is to build what I call a line-item rubric. Line-item rubrics supply multiple criteria for evaluation. Below is a blank frame for a line-item rubric and then a sample rubric for poetry writing. The unique features of line-item rubrics are that criteria statements are listed according to writing conventions and content, a numeric value is provided for quantative data collection, and there is a space for comments and point totals.

The advantages of using this rubric format begin with the ease of developing an assessment tool that is specifically tailored to the needs of the student and the content demands of the genre. The teacher can reference appropriate statements from content standards as criteria. Further, scoring the rubric requires only a check mark next to the criteria statement, which speeds up the assessment process. This format also facilitates communication with the student by providing a clear indication of the areas of strengths and needs.

Line-Item Rubric Assessment

Assessment Criteria	Evaluation				
Conventions	*4*	*3*	*2*	*1*	*Points and Comments*
•					
•					
•					
•					
•					
Content	*4*	*3*	*2*	*1*	*Points and Comments*
•					
•					
•					
•					
•					

Evaluation Key

4 = Outstanding, 3 = Satisfactory, 2 = Needs Improvement, 1 = Incomplete, Off Topic, or Missing

Sample Line-Item Rubric Assessment

Assessment Criteria	Evaluation				
Conventions	*4*	*3*	*2*	*1*	*Points and Comments*
• Spells key words correctly		X			*Check spelling of "turtle, stream, deeply"*
• Appropriate capitalization	X				
• Uses ending punctuation	X				*Be sure to maintain the syllable count on line #6*
• Follows poetry form		X			
Content	*4*	*3*	*2*	*1*	*Points and Comments*
• Meaningful response to a story	X				
• Conveys personal expression	X				*Only one metaphor, consider more use of simile. Need more description, use richer adjectives*
• Creates an image with metaphor			X		
• Uses descriptive words		X			

Evaluation Key

4 = Outstanding, 3 = Satisfactory, 2 = Needs Improvement, 1 = Incomplete, Off Topic, or Missing

Writing conference log. As students engage in process writing, they need to conference with a teacher. Several tasks take place during a writing conference: the teacher reviews the writing for format, content, and errors; consults with the student about the strengths and the needs of the writing; notes next steps to take; and records observations for assessment purposes. The value of a writing conference log is that it facilitates all of the above tasks on a single sheet of paper that is filed with the student's portfolio as a record of consultation for assessment purposes.

The features of the writing conference log are as follows: spaces to identify the student, the working title, and the genre of the writing; a column to record the date of each conference; ample space to write specific comments about the work; and specific rubric criteria for easy reference.

The student keeps the writing conference log clipped to the current draft of the writing. Each time the student meets with the teacher, the date is recorded and comments are added. The rubric space is initially blank so that a uniquely tailored rubric can be developed with the student's input. When the process writing is complete, the teacher takes the writing conference log and keeps it on file in the student's portfolio.

Another function of the writing conference log is as a means of communication with the student's family about work that needs to be done at home. By reviewing the writing conference log, a parent can get a clear idea of the nature of the writing, the rubric requirements, and special instructions from the teacher. Parents can also be invited to write comments on the log to further involve them in their child's writing process. A blank frame is provided below, followed by a sample sheet that is filled in.

Writing Conference Log and Rubric

Student's Name _____

Working Title and Genre _____

Conference Date(s)	Editorial Notes

Assessment Criteria Rubric
Language Conventions
•   •
Content Understanding
•   •

Sample Writing Conference Log and Rubric

Student's Name _____ Josue V. _____

Working Title and Genre ____ "The Knights of Queen Califa"/Fantasy _____

Conference Date(s)	Editorial Notes
7/30	*Your first sentence catches the reader's attention. Consider following with a few sentences that set the location of the story. Think about setting. Provide descriptive details.*
8/2	*The setting is clear and detailed. The characters need some background. Ask yourself these questions: Where did the main character come from? How long has he been a knight? Why is he opposed to the other knights? Who is he related to? What happened in the past to set the knights against each other?*
8/6	*Clearly state the problem that needs to be solved in the fourth paragraph.*
8/9	*Check the marked words for spelling. I see "rescued" misspelled several times.*
8/12	*Take out the marked sentences, they derail the story. Clarify who was saved from the fire. Not all characters are accounted for.*

Assessment Criteria Rubric
Language Conventions
• Interesting lead sentence • Minimum 5 paragraphs • Observes conventions of spelling and grammar
Content Understanding
• Fantasy story with a magical event or creature • Must include a setting/characters/problem/solution story line

Writing Assessment Tools Appropriate for Early Advanced and Advanced English Language Learners

When students are active participants in the assessment process, they become more self-directed and begin to look at their own writing with a more critical eye. Early advanced and advanced ELLs can benefit from each of the previous assessment tools. They can also benefit from active participation in assessing each other's work with rubric partners and developing rubrics.

Rubric partners. Utilizing rubric partners is a strategy that actively involves students in attending to the criteria of the rubric assessment. This is an efficient way to get all students to help each other improve their writing.

1. Prior to the drafting stage of the writing process, group students with partners. If you have an odd number in your class, group students in small groups of three.
2. Review the criteria statements for conventions and content of the writing.
3. Model how to provide critical feedback. Give the students catchphrases to use such as the following:

    "Note the first criteria statement in the rubric about . . ."

    "Consider . . ."

    "I saw three spelling errors . . ."

    "I would write it this way . . ."

    Remind students to be very courteous at this time. No degrading or insulting remarks are to be tolerated.
4. Set a timer for an allotment of writing time (suggested allotment 15 to 20 minutes).
5. When the timer expires, instruct students to stop writing and meet with their rubric partners.
6. Ask students to read aloud their unfinished draft to their partner(s).
7. Partners are instructed to refer to the rubric to provide critical feedback about the writing.
8. Once each student has received critical feedback, they return to writing their drafts. (Repeat steps 4 through 8 as needed.)

This strategy has numerous benefits. It reduces the number of times that a teacher must remind students to attend to the criteria for the writing. It utilizes the whole group for assessment. It also prepares students to evaluate their own and each other's work. They practice asking themselves, "Did I meet the rubric criteria? What do I need to do to improve this writing?"

Self-generated rubrics. A very high level of participation in writing assessment is to include the students in generating their own rubrics. Self-generated rubrics is a recommended strategy for students who are highly familiar with the design and function of rubrics. As part of the writing process, consult with students about their own writing and how to evaluate it. Give them a blank rubric frame or a rubric with only a few criteria written in. Their task is to consider what would be important criteria for their own writing, to state that criteria on the rubric in terms of conventions and content, and then to hold themselves accountable to meet their own criteria. The Writing Conference Log is an ideal vehicle for this activity. It provides a frame for writing the rubric and is kept clipped to the student's writing for easy reference. To get specific language for a rubric, refer to the next section on suggested rubric language.

Suggested rubric language. There is no single rubric that can be used for writing assessment. Apart from the standard conventions of spelling, grammar, and punctuation, each genre employs unique formats for conventions and content. Provided below is sample rubric language that can be used across levels of proficiency and with specific genres of writing. The differentiation between early intermediate/intermediate and early advanced/advanced is dictated by two essential factors. The first factor is length and complexity of the writing required by the teacher, such as requiring that early intermediate students write one as opposed to three paragraphs, or that intermediate students use more details. The second factor is whether or not the students had been provided sufficient instruction in one or more of the criteria areas. For example, with narrative writing an early advanced student may need more instruction in establishing a point of view. In that case the teacher could choose to leave the rubric criteria in place, but weigh other criteria more heavily in the evaluation until it was determined that the student could demonstrate sufficient mastery of the requirement.

The following is suggested rubric language across four genres of writing: narrative, expository, biographical, and persuasive. The rubrics provide language for conventions and content with the exception of expository writing in which the content is established according to the selected topic.

Narrative Writing Rubric	*Beginning*	*Early Intermediate/ Intermediate*	*Early Advanced/ Advanced*
Conventions	• Dictates and copies one or more paragraphs • Logical sequence of events • Uses a graphic organizer	• Utilizes story elements (setting, plot, conflict) • One or more paragraphs • Logical sequence of events • Appropriate formats for action and dialog	• Utilizes story elements (setting, plot, conflict) • Multiple paragraphs • Chronological or thematic sequence of events • Appropriate formats for action and dialog
Content	• Identifies a setting • Selects important events • Describes events in order	• Establishes a point of view • Setting described as time and place • Shows, rather than tells, events • Articulates the significance of the experience	• Establishes a point of view • Setting described with rich details • Shows, rather than tells, events • Articulates a lesson learned, moral, or the significance of the experience

Expository Writing Rubric	*Beginning*	*Early Intermediate/ Intermediate*	*Early Advanced/ Advanced*
Conventions (Content varies according to topic)	• Topic sentence • One paragraph dictated or written with assistance • Ideas/events in sequence or chronological order • Concluding sentence	• Topic sentence • Multiple paragraph organization • Ideas/events in sequence or chronological order • Conclusion summarizes ideas	• Topic sentence • Five-paragraph organization • Ideas/events in sequence or chronological order • Provides details and transitions • Conclusion summarizes ideas

Biographical Writing Rubric	*Beginning*	*Early Intermediate/ Intermediate*	*Early Advanced/ Advanced*
Conventions	• Dictates and copies description of a selected person • Begins with a statement about the person	• Provides an opening sentence • Essay of one or more paragraphs • Chronological or thematic sequence of events	• Captivating opening sentence • Multiple paragraph essay • Chronological or thematic sequence of events

(continued)

Biographical Writing Rubric	Beginning	Early Intermediate/ Intermediate	Early Advanced/ Advanced
	• Uses a time line to order events	• Details supplied • Provides a conclusion	• Details supplied • Conclusion is well supported
Content	• Selects a significant person as subject • Identifies important events in person's life • Describes events in order	• Establishes the importance of the person • Cites an information source	• Establishes the importance of the person • Cites sources of information • Takes a stance about the person's contributions or detractions

Persuasive Writing Rubric	Beginning	Early Intermediate/ Intermediate	Early Advanced/ Advanced
Conventions	• Dictates an opinion • Formulates a topic sentence • Uses a graphic organizer to show relationship of evidence to argument for opinion	• Opinion stated in topic sentence • Essay of one or more paragraphs • Evidence and argument(s) match • Provides a conclusion	• Opinion stated in topic sentence • Multiple paragraph essay • Evidence and arguments match • Conclusion is well supported
Content	• Chooses a side given two arguments • States an opinion • Identifies one or more reasons for the opinion	• States an opinion • Supports opinion with one or more arguments • Provides evidence	• Well-founded opinion • Supports opinion with at least three arguments • Each argument is supported by evidence

References

Graves, D. (1984). *Writing: Teachers and children at work*. Exeter, NH: Heinemann.

Vygotsky, L. S. (1978). *Mind and society*. Cambridge, MA: Harvard University Press.

Index